Operating Systems

Dr. Sai Krishna

London·Istanbul·Moscow·Delhi·Jakarta

Operating Systems
by Dr. Sai Krishna

Published by Glimmer Publishing Ltd. Ground Floor 2, Woodberry Grove, London, N12 0DR, England.

Glimmer books may be purchased for educational, business, or sales promotional use. Online editions are also available for most titles (*http://glimmerpublishing.com*). For more information, contact our corporate sales department: *sales@glimmerpublishing.com*.

February 2018: First Edition

See *http://glimmerpublishing.com/978-1-78902-011-3* for release details

The Glimmer logo is a registered trademark ofGlimmer Publishing Ltd.
The cover image source: iharrow.org.uk
Cover design by Glimmer Publishing Ltd.

ISBN: 978-1-78902-011-3

SYLLABUS

Introduction, Quality of Operation system, feature of operating system, architecture of operating systems, operations of OS, classification of OS, types of processing, types of OS, timesharing, personal computing

Process and its state, types of scheduler, scheduling performance criteria, scheduling algorithm, virtual memory, paging, demand paging, process creation, page replacement and its algorithm, allocation of frames, thrashing, Pre paging, page size, inverted page table.

Synchronization, mutual exclusion, semaphores, classical problems, introduction of deadlock, deadlock characterization, deadlock avoidance.

Memory management, address binding, logical and physical address space, dynamic loading, linking and shared libraries, swapping, Contiguous Memory allocation, memory protection and allocation, fragmentation, paging, segmentation, maltics, file concept, attributes, operations, access methods, directory structure, file-system mounting, file sharing, protection.

Security, authentication, threats, securing systems, intrusion detection, cryptography and computer security.

UNIX commands.

TABLE OF CONTENTS

UNIT 1

INTRODUCTION TO OPERATING SYSTEMS

1.1 What is an Operating System

An OS or Operating System is a software package, which allows the computer to function. Operating systems is essentially the body of the computer. An operating System is a system, which may be viewed as an organization collection of software consisting of procedures for operating a computer and providing an environment for execution of programs. The primary objective of an operating system is to make computer system convenient to use and utilize computer hardware in an efficient manner. An operating system is a large collection of software, which manages resources of the computer system, such as memory, processor, and file system and input/output devices. It keeps track of the status of each resource and decides who will have a control over computer resources. It acts as an interface between users and the hardware of a computer system.

A computer, without any software, is essentially of no use. It is with its software that it can store, process and retrieve information. Computer software can be divided into two kinds: **system programs** - those that manage the operation of the computer itself, and **application programs**- those that perform the actual work the user wants. The most fundamental system program is the **operating system**- it controls all the computer's resources and provides the base upon which the application programs can be written. It is a program that acts as an intermediary between a user of a computer and the computer hardware; it controls and coordinates the use of this hardware among its users. An operating system is the program that controls all the other parts of a computer system both the hardware and the software.

There are many important reasons for studying operating systems. Some of them are:

i.User interacts with the computer through operating system in order to accomplish his task since it is his primary interface with a computer.

i.   It helps user to understand the inner function of a computer very closely.

i.   Many concepts and techniques found in operating system have general applicability in other applications.

OS Function can be classified into:

i.Resource allocation and related function: - The resource allocates resource for user by users of a computer system. The resource can be dividing into system-provided resource like CPU's, memory areas and IO devices, or user created resource like file, which are entrusted to the OS. Allocation of system resource in driven by its consideration of efficiency of resource utilization.

i.User interface function.

The resource allocation function implements resource sharing by the users of a computer system.

1.2 Qualities of Operating System
- Usability:
  - Robustness: -accept all valid input without error, and gracefully handles all invalid inputs.

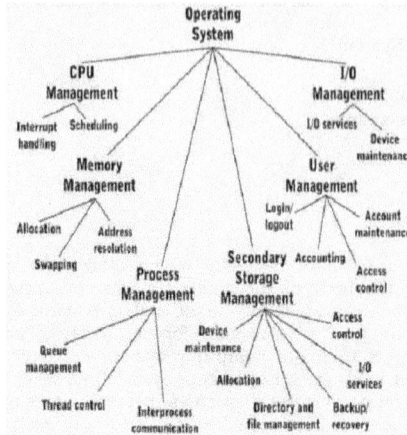

  - Consistency: - E.g., if "-" means options flags in one place, it means it in another. Key idea: **conventions**. Concept: The Principle of Least Astonishment.
  - Proportionality: - Simple, cheap and frequent things are easy. Also, expensive and disastrous things (ram *) are hard.
  - Forgiving: -Errors can be recovered from. Reasonable error messages. Example from "rm"; UNIX vs. TOPS.
  - Convenient: - Not necessary to repeat things, or do awkward procedures to accomplish things. Example copying a file took a batch job.
  - Powerful: - Has high-level facilities.
  - Facilities
- Sufficient for intended use.
- Complete
- Appropriate.
- Costs
  - Want low cost and efficient services.
  - Good algorithms: -Make use of space/time tradeoffs, special hardware.
  - Low overhead: - Cost of doing nothing should be low. E.g., idle time at a terminal.
  - Low maintenance cost: -System should not require constant attention.
  - Adaptability
- Tailored to the environment: - Support necessary activities. Do not impose unnecessary restrictions. What are the things people do most -- make them easy.
- Changeable over time: -Adapt as needs and resources change. E.g., expanding memory and new devices, or new user population.

Extensible: -Adding new facilities and features - which look like the old ones.

1.3 Feature of Operating System

- **Multi-User:** Allows two or more users to run programs at the same time. Some operating systems permit hundreds or even thousands of concurrent users.
- **Multi Processing:** Supports running a program on more than one CPU.
- **Multi Tasking:** Allows more than one program to run concurrently.
- **Multithreading:** Allows different parts of a single program to run concurrently.

- **Real time:** Responds to input instantly. General-purpose operating systems, such as DOS and UNIX, are not real-time.

The operating system is also responsible for security, ensuring that unauthorized users do not access the system. All desktop computers have operating systems. The primary operating systems in use are the many versions **Windows (95, 98, NT, ME, 2000, XP)**, the many

Versions of UNIX(Solaris, Linux etc.) and the **Macintosh O.S.** There are also hundreds of other operating systems available for special-purpose applications, including specializations for mainframes, robotics, manufacturing, real-time control systems and so on. Some main feature are fallowing:

- Oversees all hardware resources and allocates them to user and applications as   needed.
- Performs many low-level tasks on behalf of users and application programs.
- Provides a way for users to interact with the computer.

1.4 Architecture of operating systems

- Command Layer – the user's interface to the operating system.

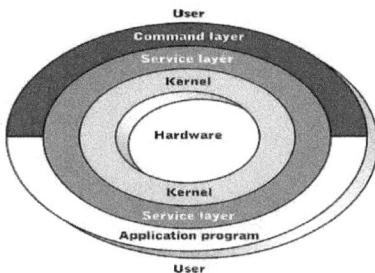

- Service Layer – contains a set of functions called by application programs and the command layer.
- Kernel – manages resources and directly interacts with computer hardware.

1.5 Operation of operating system

Resource Management/Allocation
Primary resources being managed:
- CPU - determine which process the CPU works on.
- Main memory - determine which processes can utilize which memory locations.

Extended Machine and Resource Manager

Extended Machine: The **Architecture** (instruction set, memory organization, I/O, and bus structure) of most computers at the machine Language level is primitive and awkward to program, especially for input/output. The program that hides the truth about the hardware from the programmer and presented a nice, simple view of named files that can be read and written is, of course, the operating system. The function of the operating system is to present the user with the equivalent of an **extended machine** or **virtual machine** that is easier to program than the underlying hardware.

Resource Manager: Operating system as primarily providing its users with a convenient interface are a top-down view. An alternative, button-up, view holds that the Operating system is there to manage all the pieces of a complex system. In short, this view of the operating system holds that its primary task is to keep track of who is using which resource, to grant resource requests, to account for usage, and to mediate conflicting requests from different programs and users.

Device Management
The path between the operating system and virtually all hardware not on the computer's motherboard goes through a special program called a **driver**. Much of a driver's function is to be the translator between the electrical signals of the hardware subsystems and the high-level programming languages of the operating system and application programs. Drivers take data that the operating system has defined as a file and translate them into streams of bits placed in specific locations on storage devices, or a series of laser pulses in a printer.

Because there are such wide differences in the hardware controlled through drivers, there are differences in the way that the driver programs function, but most are run when the device is required, and function much the same as any other process. The operating system will frequently assign high-priority blocks to drivers so that the hardware resource can be released and readied for further use as quickly as possible. One reason that drivers are separate from the operating system is so that new functions can be added to the driver and thus to the hardware subsystems - without requiring the operating system itself to be modified, recompiled and redistributed. Through the development of new hardware device drivers, development often performed or paid for by the manufacturer of the subsystems rather than the publisher of the operating system, input/output capabilities of the overall system can be greatly enhanced. Managing input and output is largely a matter of managing **queues** and **buffers**, special storage facilities that take a stream of bits from a device, perhaps a keyboard or a serial port, hold those bits, and release them to the CPU at a rate slow enough for the CPU to cope with. This function is especially important when a number of processes are running and taking up processor time. The operating system will instruct a buffer to continue taking input from the device, but to stop sending data to the CPU while the process using the input is suspended. Then, when the process needing input is made active once again, the operating system will command the buffer to send data.

This process allows a keyboard or a modem to deal with external users or computers at a high speed even though there are times when the CPU can't use input from those sources. Managing all the resources of the computer system is a large part of the operating system's function and, in the case of real-time operating systems, may be virtually all the functionality required. For other operating systems, though, providing a relatively simple, consistent way for applications and humans to use the power of the hardware is a crucial part of their reason for existing.

UNIT 2

Classification of Operating Systems

2.1 EVOLUTION OF OPERATING SYSTEMS

An operating system may processes its task serially(sequentially)or concurrently(several task simultaneously).It means that the resources of computer system may be dedicated to a single program until its completion or they may be allocated among several programs in different stages of execution. The feature of operating system to execute multiple programs in interleaved fashion or different time cycles is called as multiprogramming system.

2.1.1 Serial processing

Programming in 1's and 0's(machine language) was quite common for early computer system. Instruction and data used to be fed into the computer by means of consol switches or perhaps through a hexadecimal keyboard. Programs used to be started by loading the program computer register with the address of first instruction of a program and its result (program) used to be examined by the contents of various registers and memory locations of the machine. Therefore, programming in this style caused a low utilization of both users and machine.
Advent of input/output devices, such as punch cards paper tape and language translators (compiler/Assemblers) brought a significant step in computer system utilization. Program started being coded into object (binary code) by translator and then automatically gets loaded into memory by program called loader. After transferring a control to the loaded program, the execution of a program begins and its result gets displayed or printed. Once in memory, the program may be re-run with a different set of input data.

The process of development and preparation of a program in such environment is slow and cumbersome due to serial processing and numerous manual processing. In a typical sequence first the editor is called to create a source code of user program written in programming language, translator is called to covert a source code into binary code and then finally loader is called to load executable program into main memory for execution. If syntax errors are detected, the whole process must be restarted from the beginning.

2.1.2 Batch Processing

The next logical step in the evolution of operating system was to automate the sequencing of operations involved in program execution and in the mechanical aspects of program development. Jobs with similar requirement were batched together and run through the computer as a group. For example, suppose the operator received one FORTRAN program one COBOL, program and another FORTRAN program. If he runs them in that order, he would have to set up for FORTRAN program and finally FORTRAN program again. If he runs the two FORTRAN program as a batch, however he could set up only for FORTRAN thus saving operator's time.
Batching similar jobs brought utilization of system resources quit a bit. But there were still

Problems. For example, when a job is stopped, the operator would have to notice that fact that fact by observing the console, determine why the program stopped and then load the card reader or paper tape reader with the next job and restart the computer. During this transition from one job to the next, the CPU sat idle.

To overcome this idle time, a small program called a resident monitor was created which is always resident in the memory. It automatically sequenced one job to another job. **Resident monitor** acts according to the directives given by a programmer through **control cards** which contain information like marking of job's beginning and endings, commands for loading and executing programs etc. These commands belong to job control language.

2.1.3 Multiprogramming

A single user cannot always keep CPU or I/O device busy at all. Multiprogramming offers a more efficient approach to increase system performance. In order to increase the resource utilization. System supporting multiprogramming approach allows more than utilization. System supporting to utilize CPU time at any moment. More number of programs competing for system resources better will be resource utilization.

Multiprogramming has been employed to increase the resource utilization of a computer system and to support multiple simultaneously interactive users(terminals).

2.2 Types of operating system

2.2.1 Single-user, single tasking

(Single user, OS allows only one application to run at a time - e.g., DOS). As the name implies, this operating system is designed to manage the computer so that one user can effectively do one thing at a time. The **Palm O.S.** for Palm handheld computers is a good example of a modern single-user, single-task operating system.

2.2.2 Single-user, multi-tasking

(one user, OS allows multiple applications to run at a time - e.g., Windows98). This is the type of operating system most people use on desktop and laptop computers today. **Windows 98** and the **Mac O.S.** are both examples of an operating system that will let a single user have several programs in operation at the same time. For example, it's entirely possible for a Windows user to be writing a note in a word processor while downloading a file from the Internet while printing the text of an e-mail message.

2.2.3 Multi-user, multi-tasking

(multiple users, multiple applications - e.g., Unix, Linux). A multi-user operating system allows many different users to take advantage of the computer's resources simultaneously. The operating system must make sure that the requirements of the various users are balanced, and that each of the programs they are using has **sufficient and separate resources** so that a problem with one user doesn't affect the entire community of users. **Unix, VMS**, and **mainframe operating systems**, such as **MVS**, are examples of multi-user operating systems. It's important to differentiate here between multi-user operating systems and single-user operating systems that support networking. **Windows 2000** and **Novell Netware** can each support hundreds or thousands of networked users, `but the operating systems themselves aren't true multi-user operating systems. The system administrator is the only user for Windows 2000 or Netware. The network support and the entire remote user logins the network enables are, in the overall plan of the operating system, a program being run by the **administrative user**.

2.2.4 Real-Time operating System

instruments and industrial systems. An RTOS typically has very little user-interface capability, and no end-user utilities, since the system will be a sealed box when delivered for use. A very important part of an RTOS is managing the resources of the computer so that a particular operation executes in precisely the same amount of time every time it occurs. In a complex machine, having a part move more quickly just because system resources are available may be just as catastrophic as having it not move at all because the system is busy.

Computer software can be divided into two main categories: application software and system software. According to Brookshear (1997), "*application software consists of the programs for performing tasks particular to the machine's utilization. Examples of application software include spreadsheets, database systems, desktop publishing systems, program development software, and games.*" Application software is generally what we think of when someone speaks of computer programs. This software is designed to solve a particular problem for users. On the other hand, system software is more transparent and less noticed by the typical computer user. This software "***provides a general programming environment in which programmers can create specific applications to suit their needs. This environment provides new functions that are not available at the hardware level and performs tasks related to executing the application program***". System software acts as an interface between the hardware of the computer and the application software that users need to run on the computer. The diagram below illustrates the relationship between application software and system software.

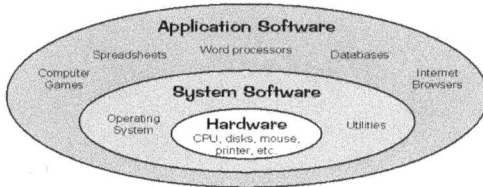

The most important type of system software is the operating system. According to Webopedia, an operating system has three main responsibilities:

1. Perform basic tasks, such as recognizing input from the keyboard, sending output to the display screen, keeping track of files and directories on the disk, and controlling peripheral devices such as disk drives and printers.
2. Ensure that different programs and users running at the same time do not interfere with each other.
3. Provide a software platform on top of which other programs (i.e., application software) can run.

The first two responsibilities address the need for managing the computer hardware and the application programs that use the hardware. The third responsibility focuses on providing an interface between application software and hardware so that application software can be efficiently developed. Since the operating system is already responsible for managing the hardware, it should provide a programming interface for application developers. Identifies four common types of operating system strategies on which modern operating systems are built: batch, timesharing, personal computing, and dedicated. **"The favored strategy for any given computer depends on how the computer is to be used, the cost-effectiveness of the strategy implementation in the application environment, and the general state of the technology at the time the operating system is developed."**

2.2.5 Batch

This strategy involves reading a series of jobs (called a batch) into the machine and then executing the programs for each job in the batch. This approach does not allow users to interact with programs while they operate.

2.2.6 Timesharing

This strategy supports multiple interactive users. Rather than preparing a job for execution ahead of time, users establish an interactive session with the computer and then provide commands, programs and data, as they are needed during the session.

2.2.7 Personal computing

This strategy supports a single user running multiple programs on a dedicated machine. Since only one person is using the machine, more attention is given to establishing predictable response times from the system.
This strategy is quite common today because of the popularity of personal computers.
Dedicated: - **This strategy supports real-time and process control systems. These are the types of systems, which control satellites, robots, and air-traffic control. The dedicated strategy must guarantee certain response times for particular computing tasks or the application is useless.**

UNIT 3

Process Management

3.1 Introduction

An operating system executes a variety of programs, Batch system – jobs, Time-shared systems, user programs or tasks. Textbook uses the terms *job* and *process* almost
interchangeably. Process – a program in execution; process execution must progress in sequential fashion. A process includes: program counter, stack, data section.

3.2 Definition and concept of Process

Process Management concerns the control of programs within the system. We use the term *process* to refer to a program that is loaded into computer memory and is being executed i.e. is utilizing CPU time. Recall that only the operating system can allocate system resources, so the process will execute in either user mode or system mode (system mode has direct access to resources).
  In order for different user processes to exist, the operating system must be able to *create* and *delete* both user and system processes. Process creation entails allocating memory into which a program is loaded before it is added to the list of processes to run. Process deletion entails its removal from the list of processes to run, and its resources are reclaimed by the operating system. Recall that, historically, one of the justifications for having multiple programs executing in a system was to avoid CPU idleness. Thus, we see modern operating systems being able to *suspend* one process while moving on to *resume* some other process.
Processes must be coordinated e.g. when the operating system finishes some I/O, it must be able to indicate that a suspended process waiting on this I/O can now resume. Process *synchronization* provides this mechanism. Processes must communicate e.g. some I/O work conducted by the operating system must be able to return data to a user process. Process *communication* provides this mechanism. It is possible for processes, which are sharing resources and/or exchanging data to become "confused" e.g. two processes wanting to use a resource might both be suspended because they are waiting for the other process to take its turn (like when two people are both waiting for each other to use an entrance). A mechanism for *deadlock* handling is provided.
All run able software on the computer, often including the operating system, is organized into number of sequential process. Conceptually, each process has its own virtual CPU. In reality, of course, the real CPU switches back or forth from process to process, but to understand the system, it is much easier to think about a collection of processes running in parallel than to try to

10

keep track of how the CPU switching from the program to program. This rapid switching back and forth is called multiprogramming.

One program counter   **Four program counters**

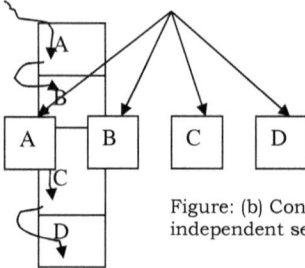

Process switching

Figure: (b) Conceptual model of four independent sequential model

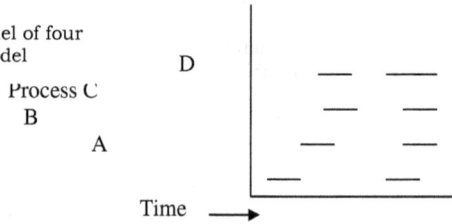

Figure: (a) Multiprogramming of four process

Figure: (c) Only one program is active. At any instance.

3.3 ProcessState

Although each process is an independent entity, with its own program counter and internal state, process often need to interact with other process. One process may generate some output that another process uses as a input.

A process is more than the program code. It also include the current activity, as represent by the value of the program counter and the processor's registers. Two process may be associated with same program.

The operating system is responsible for managing all the processes that are running on a computer and allocated each process a certain amount of time to use the processor. In addition, the operating system also allocates various other resources that processes will need such as computer memory or disks. To keep track of the state of all the processes, the operating system maintains a table known as the *process table*. Inside this table, every process is listed along with the resources the processes are using and the current state of the process. Processes can be in one of three states: running, ready, or waiting. The running state means that the process has all the resources it need for execution and it has been given permission by the operating system to use the processor. Only one process can be in the running state at any given time. The remaining processes are either in a waiting state (i.e., waiting for some external event to occur such as user input or a disk access) or a ready state (i.e., waiting for permission to use the processor). In a real operating system, the waiting and ready states are implemented as queues, which hold the processes in these states. The animation below shows a simple representation of the life cycle of a process

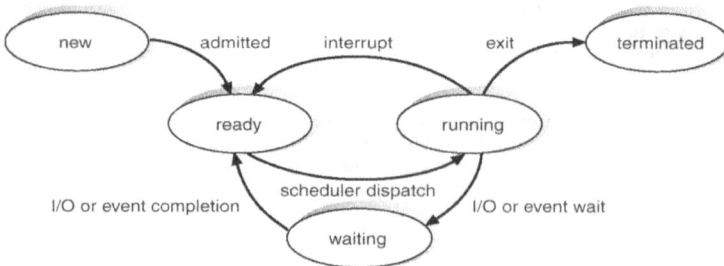

As a process executes, it changes *state.*
 a) **New:** The process is being created.

b) **Running**: Instructions are being executed.
c) **Waiting**: The process is waiting for some event to occur.
d) **Ready**: The process is waiting to be assigned to a process.
e) **Terminated**: The process has finished execution

3.4 Process Scheduling

CPU scheduling is the basis of multiprogrammed operating systems. By switching the CPU among processes, the operating system can make the computer more productive. Here, we introduce the basic scheduling concepts and discuss in great length about various CPU scheduling algorithms. Given a sequence of CPU and I/O bursts, you should be able to apply any of the above scheduling algorithms to it. You should also be able to compare these algorithms in terms of efficiency for a given class of processes (e.g., CPU or I/O-bound processes).
If there are several run able jobs, the operating system has to decide which job to run next, a process known as *Process Scheduling*. In the old days, when computers ran batch jobs, this was not an issue. The computer operator simply submitted the jobs in the order that they were delivered to him or her, and each job ran to completion. We can call this algorithm First come first served, or FIFO (first in first out). However, even this primitive system had problems. Suppose there are five jobs waiting to be run. Four of the five jobs will take about ten seconds each to run, and one will take ten minutes, but the ten-minute job was submitted first. In a FIFO system, the four fast jobs will all be held up for a long time by a large job that happened to be delivered first. This permitted the operator to run jobs using a *shortest job first* algorithm. As the name implies, instead of running jobs in the order that they are delivered, the operator would search through all available jobs and run that job which had the shortest run time. This is probably the fastest job-scheduling algorithm. If there are more processes, the reset will have to wait until the CPU is free and can be rescheduled.

3.5 Types of Schedulers

The operating System must select, for scheduling purposes, processes from the queues in some fashion. The appropriate scheduler carries out the selection process. In a batch system, there are often more processes submitted than can be executed immediately. These processes are spooled to a mass-storage device.

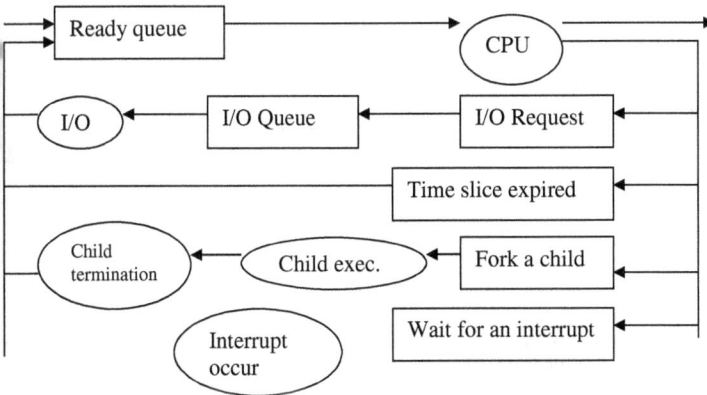

Scheduler are of basically three type on the basis of its objectives, operating environment and relationship to other schedulers in a complex operating system environment.

3.5.1 Long term scheduler: it is also called job scheduling. This determines which job shall be admitted for immediate processing.

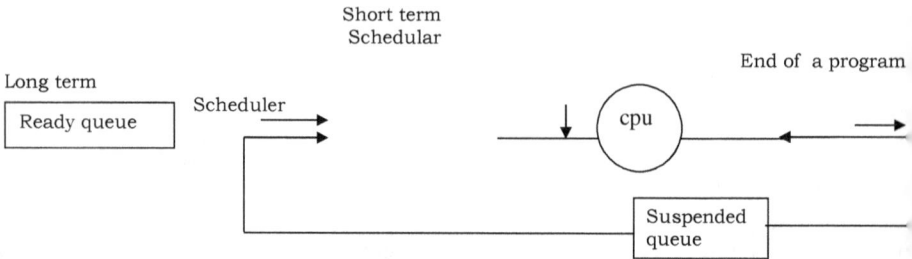

There are always more processes than CPU can be executed by operating system. These processes are kept in large storage devices like disk later processing. The long-term scheduler select processes from this pool and loads them into memory. In memory these processes belong to a **ready Queue.** Queue is a type of data structure.

3.5.2 Medium term scheduler

Most of the processes require some I/O operation. In that case, it may become suspended for I/O operation after running a while. It is beneficial to remove these process (suspended) from main memory to hard disk to make room for other processes. At some later time these process can be reloaded into memory and continued where from it was left earlier. Saving of the suspended processes is said to be swapped out or rolled out. The process is swapped in and swapped out by medium term scheduler.

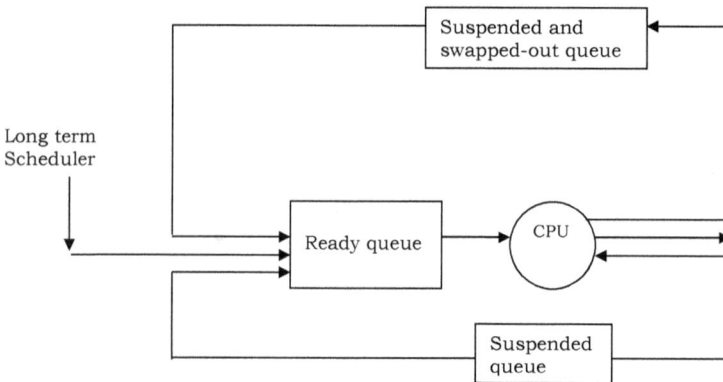

Medium term scheduler

The medium term scheduler has nothing to do with suspended processes. But the moment the suspending condition is fulfilled the medium term scheduler get activated to allocate the memory and swap in the process and make it ready for commenting CPU resources. In order to work properly, the medium term scheduler must be provided with information about the memory requirement of swapped out processes, which is usually recorded at time of swapping and stored in related process control block.

3.5.3 Short-term scheduler

It allocates processes belong to ready queue to CPU for immediate processing. Its main objective is to maximize CPU requirement. Compared to the other two scheduler it is more frequent. It must select a new process for execution quite often because a CPU execute a process only for millisecond before it goes for I/O operation. Often the short term scheduler execute a process for 10 millisecond.if it takes 1 millisecond to decide to execute a process for 10millisecond,the 1/(10+1)=9% of the CPU is being wasted simply for scheduling the work. Therefore,it must be very fast.

3.6 Scheduling Algorithms

3.6.1 First come first served scheduling

The process that requests the CPU first is allocated the CPU first. The average waiting time for FCFS policy is often quite long. Example:
Consider the following set of processes that arrive at time 0.

Process	CPU Burst Time (ms)
P1	24
P2	3
P3	3

Suppose that processes arrive in the order: P1, P2, P3, we get the result shown in the Gantt chart below:

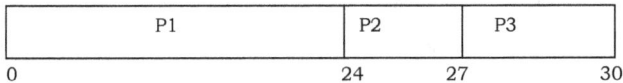

P1	P2	P3

0   24   27   30

Waiting time for P1 = 0; P2 = 24; P3 = 30
Ave. waiting time: (0 + 24 + 27) /3 = 17 ms.

If the processes arrive in the order: P2, P3, P1, then the Gantt chart is as follows:

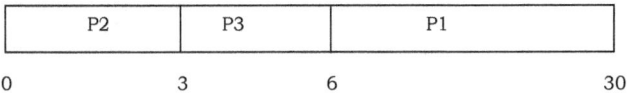

P2	P3	P1

0   3   6   30
Waiting time for P1 = 6; P2 = 0; P3 = 3
Ave. waiting time : (6 + 0 + 3)/3 = 3

Much better than the previous case, where we had a _Convoy Effect_: short process behind long process. Results in lower CPU utilization.

3.6.2 Shortest job first Scheduling

Associate with each process the length of its next CPU burst. Use these lengths to schedule the process with the shortest time. 2 schemes:
Non-preemptive - once CPU is given to the process, it cannot be preempted until it completes its CPU burst.
Preemptive - if a new process arrives with CPU burst length less than remaining time of of current executing process, preempt.

Process	CPU burst time
P1	6
P2	8
P3	7
P4	3

P4	P1	P3	

```
0        3         9              16            24
```

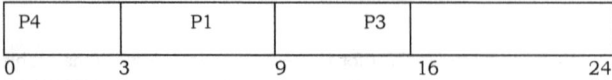

3.6.3 Priority Scheduling

The SJF is a special case of the general *priority* scheduling algorithm. A priority (an integer) is associated with each process. The CPU is allocated to the process with the highest priority (smallest integer = highest priority). Equal priority processes are scheduled in FCFS order. *Example:* The following processes arrive at time 0 in the order - P1, P2, P3, P4, P5.

Process	Burst Time	Priority
P1	10	3
P2	1	1
P3	2	3
P4	1	4
P5	5	2

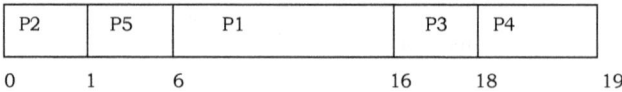

P2	P5	P1	P3	P4

```
0    1    6              16   18        19
```

The average waiting time is:
$(0 + 1 + 6 + 16 + 18)/5 = 8.2$ ms

Priority scheduling can be either preemptive or non-preemptive. A major problem with priority scheduling algorithms is *indefinite blocking* or *starvation*. Low priority processes could wait indefinitely for the CPU. A solution to the problem of starvation is *aging*. Aging is a technique of gradually increasing the priority of processes that wait in the system a long time.

3.6.4 Round Robin Scheduling

Designed for time-sharing systems. Similar to FCFS, with preemption added. Each process gets a small unit of CPU time (a time slice), usually 10 - 100 milliseconds. After time slice has elapsed, the process is preempted and added to the end of the ready queue. The ready queue can be implemented as a FIFO queue of processes. New processes are added to the tail of the queue. The scheduler picks the first process from the ready queue, sets a timer to interrupt after 1 time quantum and then dispatches the process. One of two things will happen:

The process may have a CPU burst of less than 1 time quantum, or CPU burst of the currently executing process is longer than one time quantum. In this case, the timer will go off, cause an interrupt, a context switch is then executed & the process put at the tail of the ready queue. The average waiting time under the RR scheme is often quite long. Consider the following set of processes that arrive at time 0, the time quantum is set at 4 ms:

Process	CPU Burst Time
P1	24
P2	3
P3	3

P1	P2	P3	P1	P1	P1	P1	P1

```
0    4    7    10    14    18    22    26   30
```

The average waiting time is : $17/3 = 5.66$ ms.

Performance of RR:

• If there are n processes in the ready queue at time quantum q, then each process gets $1/n$ of the CPU time in chunks of at most q time units at once. No process waits more than **(n-1) x q** time units until its next time quantum.
• The performance of RR depends on the size of q.
• At one extreme, if q is very large, RR policy is the same as FCFS policy.
• If q is very small, the RR approach is called *processor sharing*. Overhead is too high.

3.6.5 Multilevel Queue Scheduling

A multi-level queue-scheduling (MLQ) algorithm partitions the ready queue into several separate queues. Created for situations in which processes are easily classified into groups. For e.g.
✓ *foreground* (interactive) processes and
✓ *background* (batch) processes).
These two types of processes have different response-time requirements, and thus, different scheduling needs.
- The processes are permanently assigned to one queue, based on some property of the process. (e.g. memory size, priority, or type).
- Each queue has its own scheduling algorithm. For e.g. the foreground queue might be scheduled by an RR algorithm, while the background queue is scheduled by a FCFS algorithm.
- There must be scheduling between the queues. Commonly implemented as fixed-priority preemptive scheduling. I.e. foreground processes have absolute priority over the background processes, => starvation.
- Could also use a time slice algorithm where each queue gets a certain amount of CPU time which it can schedule among its processes. E.g.:
  - 80% to foreground in RR
  - 20% t o background in FCFS
  Example: An MLQ with 5 queues:

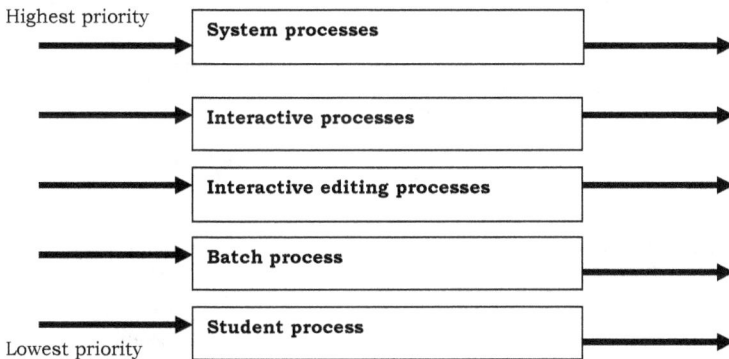

Highest priority
| System processes |
| Interactive processes |
| Interactive editing processes |
| Batch process |
| Student process |
Lowest priority

3.6.6 Multilevel feedback Queue Scheduling

So far we looked at CPU scheduling algorithms for single processor systems. If multiple CPUs exist, the scheduling problem is more complex. As with single processor systems, there is no one best solution.

Issues concerning Multiprocessor Scheduling:
With identical processors, *load-sharing* can occur. Could provide a separate queue for each processor. This could lead to a situation where one processor could be idle with an empty queue, while another processor s very busy. To prevent this situation, we could use a common ready queue. All processes enter one queue and are scheduled onto any available processor. In such a scheme, one of two scheduling approaches may be used:
a) each processor is self-scheduling => processors must be synchronized. Can't have two processors choosing the same process.

b) one processor is appointed as the scheduler for the other processors, thus creating a master-slave structure.

3.6.7 Multiple-Processor Scheduling

Some system carry this structure one step further, by having all scheduling decisions, I/O processing, and other system activities handles by one single processor-the master server. The other processors only execute user code. This asymmetric multiprocessing is far simpler than symmetric multiprocessing, because only one processor access the system data sharing. I/o bound processes may bottleneck multiprocessing is implemented first within an operating system. Typically, asymmetric multiprocessing is implemented first within an operating system, and is then upgraded to symmetric multiprocessing as the system evolves. CPU scheduling more complex when multiple CPUs are available.
• *Homogeneous processors* within a multiprocessor.
• *Load sharing*
• *Symmetric Multiprocessing (SMP)* – each processor makes its own scheduling decisions.
• *Asymmetric multiprocessing* – only one processor accesses the
      system data structures, alleviating the need for data sharing.

3.7 Real-Time Scheduling

Real-time operating systems and discussed their growing importance. real-time computing is divided into two types.

Hard real-time **systems** – required to complete a critical task within a guaranteed amount of time. Systems are required to complete a critical task within a guaranteed amount of time. A process is submitted along with a statement of the amount of time in which it needs to complete or perform I/O. the scheduler then either admits the process, guaranteeing that the process will complete on time. Hard real time system are composed of special-purpose software running on hardware dedicated to their critical process, and lack the full functionality of modern computer and operating system.

Soft real-time **computing** – requires that critical processes receive Priority over less
fortunate ones. it is less restrictive. It requires that critical processes receive priority over less fortunate ones. Although adding software real-time functionality to a time sharing system may cause an unfair allocation of resources and may result in longer delays. Soft real time systems acceptably in an environment require careful design of the scheduler and related aspect of the operating system. The system must have priority scheduling, and real time process must have the highest priority. The dispatch latency must be small. The smaller the latency, the faster a real-time process can start executing once it is runnable.

UNIT 4

INTRODUCTION TO VIRTUAL MEMORY

4.1 Introduction

Virtual memory was invented in 1959 to hide the memory hierarchy and significantly simplify programming. Now so common that no one pays much attention to it, virtual memory is one of the great engineering triumphs of the computer age.

A processor can only access memory one location at a time, so the vast majority of RAM is unused at any moment. Since disk space is cheap compared to RAM, then moving information in RAM to hard disk can greatly expand RAM space at no cost. This technique is called **virtual memory management**. Disk storage is only one of the memory types that must be managed by the operating system, and is the slowest. Ranked in order of speed, the types of memory in a computer system are:

• *High-speed cache:* This is fast, a relatively small amount of memory that are available to the CPU through the fastest connections. Cache controllers predict which pieces of data the CPU will need next and pull it from main memory into high-speed cache to speed up system performance.

• *Main memory:* This is the RAM that you see measured in megabytes when you buy a computer.

• *Secondary memory:* This is most often some sort of rotating magnetic storage that keeps applications and data available to be used, and serves as virtual RAM under the control of the operating system.

The operating system must balance the needs of the various processes with the availability of the different types of memory, moving data in blocks (called **pages**) between available memory as the schedule of processes dictates. Another way in which the memory manager enhances the ability of the operating system to support multiple process running simultaneously is by the use of virtual memory.

> *"virtual memory strategies allow a process to use the CPU when only part of its address space is loaded in the primary memory. In this approach, each process's address space is partitioned into parts that can be loaded into primary memory when they are needed and written back to secondary memory otherwise."*

Another consequence of this approach is that the system can run programs which are actually larger than the primary memory of the system, hence the idea of "virtual memory."

"Suppose, for example, that a main memory of 64 megabytes is required but only 32 megabytes is actually available. To create the illusion of the larger memory space, the memory manager would divide the required space into units called pages and store the contents of these pages in mass storage. A typical page size is no more than four kilobytes. As different pages are actually required in main memory, the memory manager would exchange them for pages that are no longer required, and thus the other software units could execute as though there were actually 64 megabytes of main memory in the machine." In order for this system to work, the memory manager must keep track of all the pages that are currently loaded into the primary memory. This information is stored in a page table maintained by the memory manager. A page fault occurs whenever a process requests a page that is not currently loaded into primary memory. To handle page faults, the memory manager takes the following steps:

1. The memory manager locates the missing page in secondary memory.
2. The page is loaded into primary memory, usually causing another page to be unloaded.
3. The page table in the memory manager is adjusted to reflect the new state of the memory.
4. The processor re-executes the instructions which caused the page fault.

Storage allocation has always been an important consideration in computer programming due to the high cost of main memory and the relative abundance and lower cost of secondary storage. Program code and data required for execution of a process must reside in main memory to be executed, but main memory may not be large enough to accommodate the needs of an entire process. Early computer programmers divided programs into sections that were transferred into main memory for a period of processing time. As the program proceeded, new sections moved into main memory and replaced sections that were not needed at that time. In this early era of computing, the programmer was responsible for devising this overlay system.
As higher level languages became popular for writing more complex programs and the programmer became less familiar with the machine, the efficiency of complex programs suffered from poor overlay systems. The problem of storage allocation became more complex.
Two theories for solving the problem of inefficient memory management emerged -- static and dynamic allocation. **Static** allocation assumes that the availability of memory resources and the memory reference string of a program can be predicted. **Dynamic** allocation relies on memory usage increasing and decreasing with actual program needs, not on predicting memory needs.
Program objectives and machine advancements in the '60s made the predictions required for static allocation difficult, if not impossible. Therefore, the dynamic allocation solution was generally accepted, but opinions about implementation were still divided. One group believed the programmer should continue to be responsible for storage allocation, which would be accomplished by system calls to allocate or de-allocate memory. The second group supported **automatic storage allocation** performed by the operating system, because of increasing complexity of storage allocation and emerging importance of multiprogramming. In 1961, two groups proposed a one-level memory store. One proposal called for a very large main memory to alleviate any need for storage allocation. This solution was not possible due to very high cost. The second proposal is known as ***virtual memory.***

Definition of Virtual Memory

Virtual memory is a technique that allows processes that may not be entirely in the memory to execute by means of automatic storage allocation upon request. The term virtual memory refers to the abstraction of separating **LOGICAL** memory--memory as seen by the process--from **PHYSICAL** memory--memory as seen by the processor. Because of this separation, the programmer needs to be aware of only the logical memory space while the operating system maintains two or more levels of physical memory space. The virtual memory abstraction is implemented by using secondary storage to augment the processor's main memory. Data is transferred from secondary to main storage as and when necessary and the data replaced is written back to the secondary storage according to a predetermined replacement algorithm. If the data swapped is designated a fixed size, this swapping is called ***paging***; if variable sizes are permitted and the data is split along logical lines such as subroutines or matrices, it is called ***segmentation***. Some operating systems combine segmentation and paging

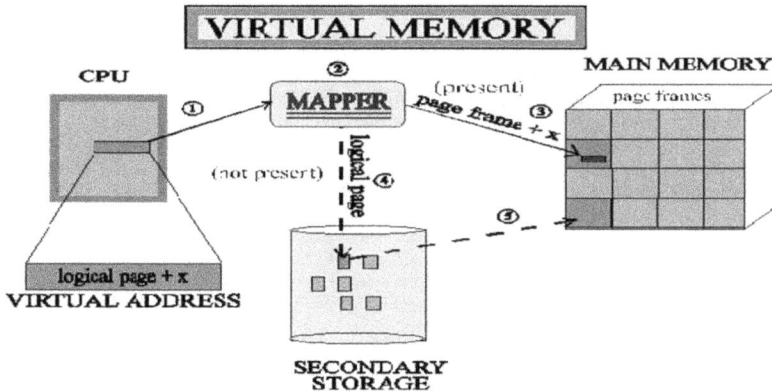

VIRTUAL MEMORY

The diagram illustrates that a program generated address (1) or "logical address" consisting of a logical page number plus the location within that page (x) must be interpreted or "mapped" onto an actual (physical) main memory address by the operating system using an address translation function or mapper(2). If the page is present in the main memory, the mapper substitutes the physical page frame number for the logical number (3). If the mapper detects that the page requested is not present in main memory, a fault occurs and the page must be read into a frame in main memory from secondary storage.

4.2 Basic Of Virtual Memory

Virtual memory is a technique that allows the execution of processes that may not be completely in memory. One major advantage of this scheme is that programs can be larger than physical memory. Further, virtual memory abstracts main memory into an extremely large, uniform array of storage, separating logical memory as viewed by the user from physical memory. This technique frees programmers from the concerns of memory – storage limitations. Virtual memory also allows processes to easily share files and address spaces, and it provides an efficient mechanism for process creation. Virtual memory is not easy to implement, however, and may substantially decrease performance if it is used carelessly. In this chapter, we discuss virtual memory in the form of demand paging, and examine its complexity and cost.

4.3 Objective

Until now, all our discussions have assumed that all programs run by the operating system fit into available memory. What if we have a program that does not? **Overlays** were the first solution to this problem. The program was split into pieces called overlays. All overlays were kept on the disk and swapped in and out of memory as needed. Overlay 0would start running first; when it was done, it would call another overlay. The problem with this approach was that the programmer would have to split the program into overlays manually. **Virtual memory** was developed thereafter that made the computer do all the work.

The motivation behind the idea is that if the combined size of the program, data and stack exceeds the amount of available physical memory, the operating system can still execute the program. Those parts of the program that are currently in use are stored in main memory; the rest on the disk. For example, a 16M program can run on a 4M machine by choosing which parts to keep in memory and which on the disk. The pieces of the program are swapped between memory and disk as required. Virtual memory can work in a multiprogramming system as well, with bits and pieces of many programs in memory.

4.4 Paging

In a system that implements virtual memory, all addresses generated by the program are virtual addresses. In a system without it, all addresses generated by the program can be put directly on the memory bus because the virtual address is the same as the physical address. With virtual memory however, the addresses go to a MMU (Memory Management Unit) that maps the virtual addresses to physical addresses. The virtual address space is divided into **pages**. These correspond to **page frames** in physical memory. Both have exactly the same size. Transfers between memory and disk are always in units of pages. Typical page sizes are anywhere between 512 bytes to 64K

Virtual memory is a technique that allows the execution of processes that may not be completely in memory. One major advantage of this scheme is that programs can be larger than physical memory. Further, virtual memory abstracts main memory into an extremely large, uniform array of storage, separating logical memory as viewed by the user from physical memory. This technique frees programmers from the concerns of memory – storage limitations. Virtual memory also allows processes to easily share files and address spaces, and it provides an efficient mechanism for process creation. Virtual memory is not easy to implement, however, and may substantially decrease performance if it is used carelessly. In this chapter, we discuss virtual memory in the form of demand paging, and examine its complexity and cost.

4.5 Demand Paging

Processes reside on secondary memory (which is usually a disk.) When we want to execute a process, we swap it into memory. Rather than swapping the entire process into memory, however, we use a lazy swapper. A lazy swapper never swaps a page into memory unless that page will be needed. Since we are now viewing process as a sequence of pages, rather than as one large contiguous address space, use of swap is technically incorrect. A swapper manipulates entire processes, whereas a pager is concerned with the individual pages of a process. We thus use pager, rather than swapper, in connection with demand paging.

4.6 Basic Concept

When a process is to be swapped in, the pager guesses which pages will be used before the process is swapped out again. Instead of swapping in a whole process, the pager brings only those necessary pages into memory.

The valid –invalid bit scheme describe in Section 9.4.4. can be used from this purpose. This time, however, when this bit is set to " valid" this value indicates that the associated page is both legal and in memory. If the bit is set to "invalid" this value indicates that the page either is not valid (that is, not in the logical address space of the process), or is valid but is currently on the disk. The page- table entry for a page that is brought into memory is set as usual, but the page-table entry for a page that is not currently in memory is simply marked invalid, or contains the address of the page on disk.

1. We check an internal table (usually kept with the process control block) for this process, to determine whether the reference was a valid or invalid memory access.
2. I f the reference was invalid, we terminate the process. If it was valid, but we have not yet brought in that page, we now page it in.
3. We find a free frame (by taking one from the free – frame list, for example).
4. We schedule a disk operation to read the desired page into the newly allocated frame.
5. When the disk read is complete, we modify the internal table kept with the process and the page table to indicate that the page is now in memory.
6. We restart the instruction that was interrupted by the illegal address trap. The process can now access the page as though it had always been in memory.

In the extreme case, we could start executing a process with no pages in memory. When the operating system sets the instruction pointer to the first instruction of the process, which is on a non- memory – resident page, the process immediately faults for the page. After this page is brought into memory, the process continues to execute, faulting as necessary until every page that it needs is in memory. At that point, it can execute with no more faults. This scheme is pure demand paging: never bring a page into memory until it is required. Theoretically, some programs may access several new pages of memory with each instruction execution (one page for the instruction and many for data), possibly causing multiple page faults per instruction. This situation would result in unacceptable system performance.

4.7 Process Creation

Paging and virtual memory can also provide for other benefits during process creation. In this section, we will explore two techniques made available by virtual memory that enhance performance creating and running processes.

Copy-on-write

Demand paging is used when reading a file from disk into memory and such files may include binary executables. However, process creation using the *fork()* system call may initially bypass the need for demand paging by using a technique similar to page sharing. This technique provides for rapid process creation and minimizes process.

Recall the *fork()* system call creates a child process as a duplicate of its parent. Traditional *fork()* worked by creating

Memory – Mapped Files

A sequential read of a file on disk using the standard system calls *open()*, *read()*, and *write()*. Every time the file is accessed requires a system call and disk access. Alternatively, we can use the virtual-memory technique discussed so far to tread file I/O as routine memory accesses. This approach is known as **memory mapping** a file, allowing a part of the virtual-address space to be logically associated with a file. Memory mapping a file is possible by mapping a disk block to a page in memory. Initial access to the file proceeds using ordinary demand paging, resulting in a page fault.

4.8 Page Replacement

When a page fault occurs, the operating system has to choose a page to remove from memory to make room for the page that has to be brought in. If the page being removed has been modified while in memory, it must be rewritten to the disk. If not, the page to be read in just overwrites the page being evicted. Many page replacement algorithms have been developed to choose the page to be replaced.

4.8.1 The Optimal Page Replacement Algorithm

This algorithm requires each page in memory to be labeled with the number of instructions that will be executed before that page is first referenced. The page with the highest label will be chosen for page replacement. If one page will not be used for instructions and another will not be used for 8 instructions, choosing the latter for replacement causes the page fault to occur later into the future than if the former was chosen. The problem with implementing this algorithm is that the operating system has no way of knowing when each page will be referenced next. The only way to implement this algorithm is by first running the program on a simulator and then using the page reference information from it to run the program on the actual algorithm

4.8.2 Not Recently Used Page Replacement Algorithm

Most systems implementing virtual memory have two bits associated with each page - a *reference bit* and a *modify bit* . The first is set when the page is read or written to. The second is set when the page is written to. Upon start up, both the bits for all pages of a process are set to 0 by the operating system. Periodically, the *reference bit* is cleared to distinguish pages that have not been referenced recently from those that have been. The *modify bit* is not cleared because that information is needed to decide whether a page needs to be written back to disk or not. Upon a page fault, the operating system divides all the pages into the following categories:
- Class 0: not referenced, not modified.
- Class 1: not referenced, modified.
- Class 2: referenced, not modified.

- Class 3: referenced, modified.

The algorithm chooses a page at random from the lowest numbered nonempty category. Note that this algorithm is different from one that would choose the least recently used page.

4.8.3 First-In, First-Out (FIFO) Page Replacement Algorithm

In this algorithm, the operating system maintains a list of all pages currently in memory, with the page at the head of the list the oldest one and the page at the tail the most recent arrival. On a page fault, the page at the head is removed and the new page added to the tail of the list. A problem with this algorithm is that it may throw out a heavily used page.

4.8.4 The Second Chance Page Replacement Algorithm

This algorithm is a modification of the FIFO algorithm. Before throwing out a page, the *reference bit* of the page is inspected. If it is not set, the page is both old and unused and it is replaced immediately. If the bit is set, the bit is cleared, the page is put onto the end of the list of pages, and its load time is updated to the current time. This is done until a page with its *reference bit* not set is found.

4.8.5 The Clock Page Replacement Algorithm

The clock algorithm keeps all the pages on a circular list in the form of a clock. A hand points to the oldest page. When a page fault occurs, the page being pointed to by the hand is inspected. If its *reference bit* is not set, the page is evicted, the new page is inserted into the clock in its place, and the hand is advanced one position. If the *reference bit* is set, it is cleared and the hand is advanced to the next page. This process is repeated until a page is found with its *reference bit* not set. This algorithm differs from the second chance algorithm only in its implementation - it avoids the problem of moving around pages in the list.

4.9 Allocation of Frames

The simplest case of virtual memory is the single-user system. Consider a single-user system with 128 KB memory composed of page of size 1 KB. Thus, there are 128 frames. The operating system may take 35KB, leaving 93 frames for the user process. Under pure system may take 35KB, leaving 93 frames for the user process.

There are many variation on this simple strategy. We can require that the operating system allocate all its buffer and table space from the free-frame list. When this space is not in use by the operating system, it can be used to support at all time. Thus, when a page fault occurs, there is a free frame available to page into. While is then written to the disk as the user process continues to execute.

4.10 Thrashing

Thrashing occurs when a system spends more time processing page faults than executing transactions. While processing page faults is necessary to in order to appreciate the benefits of virtual memory, thrashing has a negative effect on the system. As the page fault rate increases, more transactions need processing from the paging device. The queue at the paging device increases, resulting in increased service time for a page fault . While the transactions in the system are waiting for the paging device, CPU utilization, system throughput and system response time decrease, resulting in below optimal performance of a system. Thrashing becomes a greater threat as the degree of multiprogramming of the system increases. This graph shows that there is a degree of multiprogramming that is optimal for system performance CPU utilization reaches a maximum before a swift decline as the degree of

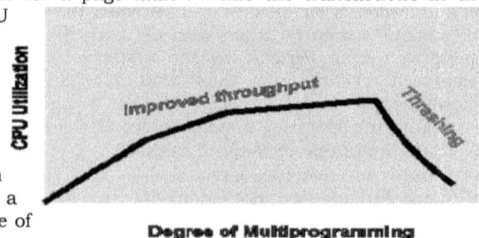

Degree of Multiprogramming

multiprogramming increases and thrashing occurs in the over-extended system. This indicates that controlling the load on the system is important to avoiding thrashing. In the system represented by the graph, it is important to maintain the multiprogramming degree that corresponds to the peak of the graph. The selection of a replacement policy to implement virtual memory plays an important part in the elimination of the potential for thrashing. A policy based on the local mode will tend to limit the effect of thrashing. In local mode, a transaction will replace pages from its assigned partition. Its need to access memory will not affect transactions using other partitions. If other transactions have enough page frames in the partitions they occupy, they will continue to be processed efficiently.

A replacement policy based on the global mode is more likely to cause thrashing. Since all pages of memory are available to all transactions, a memory-intensive transaction may occupy a large portion of memory, making other transactions susceptible to page faults and resulting in a system that thrashes.

UNIT 5

PAGING

━━

5.3 Pre paging
5.4 Page sizing
5.5 Inverted Page Table

5.1 Pre paging

An obvious of a pure demand-paging system is the large number of page faults that occur when a process is started. This situation is a result of trying to get the initial logicality into memory. The same thing may happen at other times. For instance, when a swapped-out process is restarted, all its pages are on the disk and each must be brought in by its own page fault. *Prepaging* is an attempt to prevent this high level of initial paging.

Prepaging may be an advantages in some cases. The question is simply whether the cost of Prepaging isles than the cost of servicing the corresponding page faults. It may well be the case that may of the paging brought back into the memory by Prepaging are not used.

5.2 Page sizing

The designer of an operating system for an existing machine seldom have a choice concerning the page size. However, when new machine are being designed, a design regarding the best page size must be made. As you might except, there is no single best size. Rather, there is a set of factors that support various sizes. Page sizes are invariably powers of 2, generally ranging from $512(2^9)$ to $16384(2^{14})$ bytes.

5.3 Inverted Page Table

The purpose of this form of an inverted page table was introduced. The purpose of this form of page management was to reduce the amount of physical memory that is needed to track virtual-to-physical address translation. This saving was accomplished by creating a table with one pair<process-id, page-number>.

By Keeping information which virtual-memory page is stored in each physical frame, inverted page tables reduce the amount of Physical memory needed to store this information. However, the inverted page table no longer contains complete information about the logical address space of a process, which is required if a referenced page is not currently in memory. Demand paging requires this information to process page fault.

UNIT 6

INTERPROCESS COMMUNICATION AND SYNCHRONIZATION

6.1 Introduction to Process Synchronization

In order to cooperate concurrently executing processes must communicate and synchronize. Intercrosses communication is based on the use of shared variables(variables that can be referenced by more than one process)or message passing.

Synchronization is often necessary when processes communicate. Processes are executes with unpredictable speeds. Yet to communicate one process are must perform some action such as setting the value of a variable or sending a message that the other detects. This only works if the events perform an action or detect an action are constrained to happen in that order. Thus one can view **synchronization as** a set of constraints on the ordering of events. The programmer employs a synchronization mechanism to delay execution of a process in order to satisfy such constraints.

To make this concept more clear, consider the batch operating system again. A shared buffer is used for communication between the reader process and the executor process. These processes must be synchronized so that, for example, the executer process never concerned with these two issues.

6.2 Mutual Exclusion

Processes frequently need to communicate with other process, when a user wants to read from a file, it must tell the file process what it wants, then the file process has to inform the disk process to read the required block.

Processes that are working together often share some common storage that one can read and write. The shared storage may be in main memory or it may be shared file. Each process has segment of code, called **critical section,** which accesses shared memory or files. The key issue involving shared memory or shared files is to find way to prohibit more than one process from reading and writing the shared data at the same time. In mutual exclusion –some way of making sure that if one process is executing in its **critical section, the** other processes will be excluded from doing the same thing.

Algorithm to support mutual exclusion
Module Mutex

```
Var
  P1 busy,p2 busy:Boolean;
Process p1
          Begin
            While true do
            Begin
              P1busy:=true;
                  While p2busy do {keeptesting};
                      Critical_section;
                      P1busy:=false;
                      Other_p1busy_processing
```

```
        End;{while}
    End;{p1}
Process p2;
                Begin While true do
                Begin
                  P2busy:=true;
                      While p1busy do {keeptesting};
                          Critical_section;
                          Other_p2busy_processing
End{while}
End;{p2}
{parent process}
begin{mutex}
  p1busy:=false;
  p2busy:=false
  initiate p1,p2
end{mutex}
```

p1 first sets p1busy and then tests p2busy to determined what to do next. When it finds p2busy to be false, process p1 may safely proceed to the critical section knowing that no matter how the two processes may be interleaved, process p2 is certain to find p2 busy set and to stay from the critical section. The signal change ensures mutual exclusion. But consider a case where p1 wishes to enter the critical section send sets p1busy to indicate the fact. if process p2 wishes to enter the critical section at the same time and pre-empts process p1 just before p1 test p2busy. Process p2 may set p2busy and start looping while waiting for p1 busy to become false. When control is eventually returned to process p1, it finds p2busy set and starts looping while waiting for p1busy to become false. When control is eventually returned to p1, it finds p2busy set and start looping while it waits for p2busy to become false. And so both processes are looping forever, each awaiting the other one to clear the way. In order to remove this kind of behavior, we must add another requirement to occur in our algorithm. When more than process wishes to enter the critical section, the decision to grant entrance to one of them must be made in infinite.

6.3 Semaphores

The methods all share a new property that distinguishes them from the busy-waiting methods: They depend on the ability to schedule activities. An activity that attempts to enter a region that is already occupied can be blocked, just as a process that attempts to gain a resource that is currently allocated might be blocked by the resource manager. While it waits, other activities may continue. Instead of consuming computational resources in a fruitless loop, the waiting activity only needs to suffer the cost of a context switch or two. To achieve this effect, we need to embed the Begin Region and End Region operations in the scheduler instead of building them directly on the hardware. The scheduler can also maintain a list of activities waiting to enter a region so that a fair choice can be made when conditions allow.

Our first example of this approach is to protect each group of shared variables with
a semaphore, which has the following structure:

```
1 type
2 Queue = list of Activity
3 Semaphore =
4 record
5 { all fields are initialized as shown }
6 MutEx : Lock := false;
7 Value : integer := 1;
8 Waiters : Queue := empty;
9 end;
```

The scheduler provides two operations on semaphores. The second operation is Down. Informally, Down blocks the caller if Value is 0. Otherwise, it decrements Value. Up increments Value and unblocks at most one waiting activity. The correct use of semaphores to implement mutual exclusion is simple: All regions that use the same shared variables are associated with the same semaphore. An activity that wishes to enter a region calls Down on the associated semaphore.

When the activity exits the region, it calls Up on the same semaphore. The first activity to try to enter its region succeeds, because Value is initially 1. Another activity that tries to enter while the first is still in its region will be blocked. When the first activity leaves the region, the second activity is unblocked. The Value field is always either 0 or 1. To give a more formal definition of Down and Up, we will implement them using locks as a more primitive mutual-exclusion tool.

```
1 procedure Down(var S : Semaphore);
2 begin
3 BeginRegion(S.MutEx); { use TestAndSet }
4 if S.Value = 0 then
5 Block(S.Waiters); { proceed when unblocked later }
6 else
7 S.Value := S.Value - 1;
8 end;
9 EndRegion(S.MutEx);
10 end Down;
11procedure Up(var S : Semaphore);
13 begin
14 BeginRegion(S.MutEx);
15 if not Empty(S.Waiters) then
16 UnBlock(S.Waiters) { Unblock one waiter. We continue. }
17 else
18 S.Value := S.Value + 1;
19 end;
20 EndRegion(S.MutEx);
21 end Up;
```

It is important that Down and Up be mutually exclusive. In particular, any access of the Value or the Waiters field must be atomic. That is why we use the MutEx field of each semaphore to make sure that Down and Up exclude each other. We must make sure that both Down and Up retain exclusion for only a short time; otherwise our attempt to avoid busy waiting has failed. In the simple case, Down does not find S. Value equal to 0 in line 4 and need not block in line 5. If it does block, we require that the Block routine (in the scheduler) resume some other runnable activity and that Block turn off exclusion before resumption. Block accomplishes this by calling EndRegion (S.MutEx). Block therefore needs to know which semaphore is in use; we omit this argument for clarity. UnBlock, called by Up in line 16, marks one waiting activity as runnable (for example, by placing it in a ready list). The releasing activity then continues and soon releases exclusion at line 20. When the newly runnable activity is scheduled to run, it is again given exclusion, and it finds itself running at line 5 in the Down routine. It will soon release exclusion itself in line 9. There is some controversy over whether the scheduler should switch immediately to the waiting activity that is activated in line 16. Immediate switch guarantees that whatever condition is being awaited by that activity still holds, since the Up operation has just been called and no other activity has had a chance to run. The disadvantage of an immediate switch is that it tends to increase the total number of switches. The activity that called Up is likely to call Down for a new region soon, causing it to block in any case. The Hysteresis Principle suggests that the current process should be allowed to continue. Semaphores are so useful that some operating systems provide service calls so that processes that share resources (particularly parts of virtual store) can synchronize their accesses. Four service calls are needed:

_ Semaphore Create (initial value). This call returns a new semaphore descriptor (a small integer) that the calling process may use. The semaphore structure itself is protected in the kernel and has its Value field set to the given initial value. This semaphore may be inherited by the children of the calling process so they can all

Mechanisms 269

share the same semaphore.

_ Semaphore Destroy (semaphore descriptor). This call informs the kernel that the given semaphore is no longer needed. This call is implicitly performed when the last process using a semaphore terminates. Any process waiting on a **SemaphoreDown** call receives an error return from that call.

_ SemaphoreDown(semaphore descriptor). This call performs the Down operation on the given semaphore. An error is reported if the semaphore is not associated with this process or if the semaphore is destroyed while the process is blocked waiting for it.

_ Semaphore Up (semaphore descriptor). This call performs the Up operation on the given semaphore. An error is reported if the semaphore is not associated with this process.

6.3.1 Properties of Semaphores

- They correctly implement a liberal policy of mutual exclusion among any number of activities on any number of processors. Activities interfere with each other only if they refer to the same semaphore.
- When an activity is blocked from entering its region, it does not busy wait.
- Starvation is possible unless waiters are unblocked in first-come, first-served order.
- As with all the methods we have seen so far, there is no guarantee that activities will call Down and Up at the correct times. The wrong (or no) call may be made, or the wrong semaphore may be invoked.
- A semaphore used for mutual exclusion is a serially reusable, non-preemptable resource. Its use is therefore subject to deadlock. A hierarchical order for acquiring multiple semaphores can be used to prevent deadlock.

It is easy to generalize the semaphore to allow any fixed number of activities the right to enter their region at the same time. For example, we might have seven tape drives and be willing to allow up to seven activities to access tape-drive code. To enforce this policy, we would build a semaphore for tape-drive code and initialize its value to 7 instead of 1. Semaphores allow us to implement synchronization without busy waiting. For example, we could introduce a semaphore for each arrow in the synchronization graph of Figure 8.1: AB, BE, and so on. Each semaphore would be initialized to 0. A typical activity, like E, would have this sort of code:
1 activity E:
2 Down(BE);
3 Down(DE);
4 perform E's work;
5 Up(EF);
6 Up(EH);
We don't really need so many semaphores. Instead, we could introduce just one Semaphore per activity. Again, it would be initialized to 0. When the activity finishes, it invokes Up on the semaphore as many times as there are activities waiting for this one to finish. Before an activity starts, it invokes Down on the semaphores of all the activities it needs to wait for. For example, E looks like this:
270 Concurrency Chapter 8
1 activity E:
2 Down(B);
3 Down(D);
4 perform E's work;
5 Up(E); { once for F, once for H }
6 Up(E);
One of the exercises at the end of the chapter explores another way to use semaphores to solve the same problem.
Mechanisms 271

6.3.2 Synchronization tool

Semaphore S – integer variable
can only be accessed via two indivisible (atomic) operations
    wait (S):
        while $S \leq$ 0   do   no-op;
        S--;
    signal (S):
        S++;

5.3.3 Classic Problems of Synchronization

There are a number of classic problems that appear in almost all texts on operating systems to illustrate some of the issues associated with synchronization.

The Producer - Consumer (aka Bounded Buffer) Problem

In this situation, there are two classes of processes (or threads). One class produces data of some sort, and the other consumes the data. All processes are running concurrently and asynchronously. When a producer produces some data, it puts it in a buffer. There are a finite number of buffers, and if all of the buffers are full, then the producer is blocked until a buffer becomes available.

The consumers get their data from the buffers. When a consumer is ready to consume more data, it checks to see if there is any unconsumed data in the buffers, and if there is, it consumes the data, thus emptying the buffer. If there is no data waiting to be consumed, the consumers sleep until there is data available.

Typically the data are stored in a circular buffer of size N, i.e. it has N slots for data. We will treat the buffer as a first in first out queue with the two operations Enqueue to insert an item into the buffer and Dequeue to remove an item from the buffer.

The problem is to introduce synchronization to assure that producers do not try to add data to a full buffer or that more than one consumer does not try to consume the same data.

The obvious solution is wrong; it has a fatal race condition.

```
int count = 0;  /* number of items in the buffer */
Void Producer ()            void Consumer ()
{                           {
    Data_t item;                data_t item;
    While (TRUE) {              while (TRUE) {
      Item = Produce Item ();       if (count == 0) sleep ();
      If (count == N) sleep ();     item = Dequeue ();
      Enqueue (item);              count--;
      Count++;                      if (count == N-1) wakeup (Producer);
      If (count == 1) wakeup (Consumer);    Consume Item (item);
    }                            }
}                           }
```

Make sure that you can explain why this does not work.

The solution is to have two counting semaphores, labeled full (the number of slots with data in them in the buffer) and empty (the number of empty slots in the buffer) and a mutex to make sure that only one process is accessing the buffer at a time. Recall that a semaphore has two operations, up, which increases its value and down, which decreases its value. These operations are performed atomically. If a semaphore has a value of zero, the down operation blocks until it has a non-zero value.

Here is a solution which works.

```
Semaphore empty = N;
Semaphore full = 0;
Mutex    M = Unlocked;

Void Producer ()            void Consumer ()
{                           {
    Data_t item;                data_t item;
    While (TRUE) {              while (TRUE) {
      Item = Produce Item ();       down (&full);
      Down (&empty);                lock (&M);
      Lock (&M);                    item = Dequeue ();
      Enqueue (item);              unlock (&M);
      Unlock (&M);                  up (&empty);
      Up (&full);                  Consume Item (item);
    }                            }
}                           }
```

Each producer process produces some data. Then it calls down on the empty semaphore, meaning that there is one less empty slot. This call will block if the semaphore has the value of zero. The process then locks the mutex. This will block if another process has already locked the mutex, being awakened when the mutex becomes unlocked. After doing this it stores the data that it produced into an empty slot in the buffer. There is guaranteed to be an empty slot because otherwise the down call to the semaphore empty would have blocked. After storing the data, it releases the mutex and calls up on the full semaphore, signifying that the number of full slots has been increased by one. Note that the sum of empty and full should be N, the number of slots. The consumer process is symmetrical.

The Readers and Writers Problem

Consider a file of data, such as an airline reservation system which keeps track of the reserved seats on a flight or set of flights. There are travel agents all around the country who can access this file, so there are potential issues of contention. There is no problem if many different agents want to read the file at the same time, but only one agent at a time should be able to write to the file.

Here are the rules that we want to enforce:

Any number of readers can simultaneously read the file

Only one writer at a time can write to the file

If a writer is writing, no reader can read.

No process will starve any process that wants to read or write will eventually be allowed to read or write.

Here is the solution from the text, slightly rewritten. We have a global counter Read Count which keeps track of the number of readers reading. We need two Mutex variables, Remote guards Read Count and Demote guards the database.

Int Read Count = 0; /* number of readers reading */

Mutex Remote = unlocked, Demote = unlocked;

```
Void Reader ()
{
    while (true) {
        lock(&RCMutex);
        ReadCount++;
        if (ReadCount == 1)
            lock(&DBMutex);
        unlock(&RCMutex);
        ReadDataBase();
        lock(&RCMutex);
        ReadCount--;
        if (ReadCount == 0)
            unlock(&DBMutex);
        unlock(&RCMutex);
        DoOtherStuff(); /* noncriticalsection */
    }
}
void Writer()
{
    DoOtherStuff();
    lock(&DBMutex);
    WriteDataBase();
    unlock(&DBMutex);
}
```

Unfortunately, this solution does not satisfy our criteria. It enforces mutual exclusion, but it is possible for writers to starve. If one reader is reading, as long as more readers come along and want to read, they are allowed to. Since writers are not permitted to write until there are no readers, as long as there are readers, the writers can starve.

An alternative solution is to give writers priority. If any process is waiting to write to the database, no reader is allowed to read. This solution is also unsatisfactory because it is possible for readers to starve. As long as new writers want to write, no reader ever gets to read.

Once the writer is finished writing, all of the readers that have been blocked are allowed to read. If multiple writers want to write, it is necessary to enforce alternation between readers and writers to prevent starvation. That is, after a writer has finished writing, all of the readers that have been blocked are allowed to read, but new readers that want to read are not permitted to read if there are writers waiting. Otherwise, the readers could starve.

UNIT 7

DEADLOCK

7.1 Introduction of Deadlock

With inter process communication comes the problem of *deadlock*. If a situation arises where two or more processes are all waiting for a signal from one of the other waiting processes, the processes are said to be deadlocked. Waiting and synchronization is not all sweetness and roses. Consider the European road rule, which says: on minor roads one should always wait for traffic coming from the right. If four cars arrive simultaneously at a crossroads (see Figure) then, according to the rule all of them must wait for each other and none of them can ever move. This situation is called *deadlock*. It is the *stale-mate* of the operating system world.

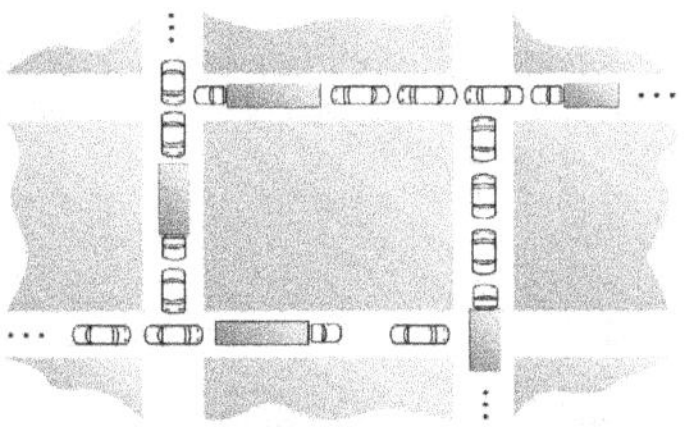

Figure 1:

A set of processes is deadlocked if each process in the set is waiting for a resource/event that only another process in the set can provide.

There is no way for the operating system to detect every conceivable deadlock condition without expending large amounts of CPU time. Thus, the only way to recover from a deadlock is to kill the processes in question. Responsibility for preventing deadlock situations is placed on the programmer. Fortunately, situations where deadlock can occur are infrequent; however, you should keep an eye out for them and try to work around them when they do occur.

7.2 System Model

Deadlock occurs when a number of processes are waiting for an event which can only be caused by another of the waiting processes.
These are the essential requirements for a deadlock:

1. **Circular waiting.** There must be a set of processes $P_1..P_n$ where P_1 is waiting for a resource or signal from P_2, P_2 is waiting for P_3 ... and P_n is waiting for P_1.
2. **Non-sharable resources.** It is not possible to share the resources or signals, which are being waited for. If the resource can be shared, there is no reason to wait.
3. **No preemption.** The processes cannot be forced to give up the resources they are holding.

There are likewise three methods for handling deadlock situations:
1. **Prevention.** We can try to design a protocol, which ensures that deadlock never occurs.
2. **Recovery.** We can allow the system to enter a deadlock state and then recover.
3. **Ostrich method.** We can pretend that deadlocks will never occur and live happily in our ignorance. This is the method used by most operating systems. User programs are

expected to behave properly. The system does not interfere. This is understandable: it is very hard to make general rules for every situation, which might arise.

7.3 Deadlock Characterization

In a deadlock, processes never finish executing and system resources are tried up, preventing other jobs from ever starting. Before we discuss the various methods for dealing with the deadlock problem, we shall describe features that characterize deadlocks.

Necessary Condition

A deadlock situation, Condition hold simultaneously in a system:

Mutual exclusion: At least one resource must be held in a non-sharable mode; that is, only one process to a time can use the resource. If another process requests that resource, the requesting process must be delayed until the resource has been released. Only one process at a time can use a resource.

Hold and wait: There must be exist a process holding at least one resource do other processes hold waiting to acquire additional resources.

No preemption: Resources cannot be preempted; that is the process holding it, after that process has completed its task can release a resource only voluntarily.

Circular wait: there exists a set $\{P_0, P_1 ... P_0\}$ of waiting processes such that P_0 is waiting for a resource that is held by P_1, P_1 is waiting for a resource that is held by P_2, P_{n-1} is waiting for a resource that is held by P_n, and P_0 is waiting for a resource that is held by P_0.

Resource-Allocation Graph

Deadlocks can be described more precisely in terms of directed graph called a system *resource-allocation graph*. This graph consist of asset of vertical V and a set of edges E.

A set of vertices V and a set of edges E. *The set of vertices V is partitioned into two different types of nodes* $P=\{P_1, P_2, P_3, ., P_n\}$, the set consisting of all resources type in the system.

A Directed Edge from process P_i to resource type R_j is denoted by $P_i \rightarrow R_j$; it signifies that process P_i requested an instance of resource type R_j and is currently waiting for that resource. A directed edge from resource type R_j to process P_i is denoted by $R_j \rightarrow P_i$ is called a *request edge;* a directed edge R_j; a directed edge $R_j \rightarrow P_i$ is called an *assignment edge.* The Resource allocation graph shown in fallowing figure

- V is partitioned into two types:
  - $P = \{P_1, P_2, ..., P_n\}$, the set consisting of all the processes in the system.
  - $R = \{R_1, R_2, ..., R_m\}$, the set consisting of all resource types in the system.
  - $E=\{P_1 \rightarrow R_1, P_2 \rightarrow R_3, R_1 \rightarrow P_2, R_2 \rightarrow P_2, R_2 \rightarrow P_1, R_3 \rightarrow P_3\}$, the set consisting of all process and resources in the System.
- Request edge – directed edge $P_1 \square R_j$
- Assignment edge – directed edge $R_j \square P_i$

The Resource allocation Graph components are fallowing:

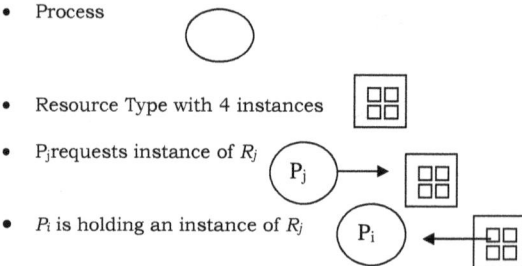

- Process

- Resource Type with 4 instances

- P_j requests instance of R_j

- P_i is holding an instance of R_j

Resource instance

- One instance of resource type R_1.
- Two instances of resource type R_2

- One instances of resource type R_3

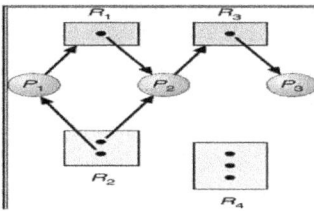

Figure 2: Resource allocation graph

- Three instances of resource type R_4

Resource allocation graph

Process states:
- Process P_1 is holding an instance of resource type R_2, and is waiting for an instance of resource type R_1.
- Process P_2 is holding an instance of R_1 and R_2, and is waiting for an instance of resource type R_3.
- Process P_3 is holding an instance of R_3.

Given the definition of a resource allocation graph. If each resource type has exactly one instance, then a cycle the cycle involves only a set of resource types, each of eadlock has occurred. Each process of which has only a single instance, then a deadlock has occurred. Each process involved in the cycle is deadlocked. In this case, a cycle in the graph is both a necessary and a sufficient condition for the existences of deadlock. If each resource type has several instances, then a cycle does not necessarily imply that a deadlock occurred. In this case, a cycle in the graph is a necessary but not a sufficient condition for the existence of deadlock. Suppose that process P_3 requests an instance of resource type R_2. Since no resource instance is currently available, a request edge $P_3 \rightarrow R_2$ is added to graph. At this point, two minimal cycles exist in the system:

$P_1 \rightarrow R_1 \rightarrow P_2 \rightarrow R_3 \rightarrow P_3 \rightarrow R_2 \rightarrow P_1$

$P_2 \rightarrow R_3 \rightarrow P_3 \rightarrow R_2 \rightarrow P_2$

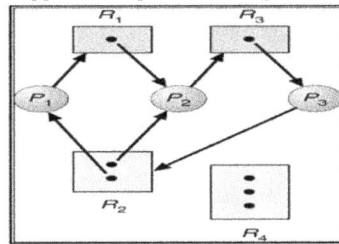

Figure 3: Resource allocation graph with a deadlock

Processes P_1, P2, and P_3 are deadlock. Process P_2 is waiting for the resource R_3, which is held by Process P_3. Process P_3, on the other hand, is waiting is waiting for either process P_1 or process P_2 to release resource R_1. Now consider the resource allocation graph. We also have a cycle

$P_1 \rightarrow R_1 \rightarrow P_3 \rightarrow R_2 \rightarrow P_1$

However, there is no deadlock. Observe that process P_4 may release its instance of resource type R_2. tha resource can them be allocated to P_3, breaking the cycle.

In *Summary*, if a resource allocation graph does not have a cycle, then the system is *not* in a deadlock state. On the other Hand, if there is a cycle, then the system may or may not be in a deadlock state.

7.4 Deadlock Prevention

Prevention establishes system policies that make it impossible for deadlock to ever take place. The way to do this is to ensure that one of the four necessary conditions cannot be satisfied.

Prevention by Forbidding Mutual Exclusion
Since mutual exclusion is necessary for correct operation in many situations, this cannot be used as a general-purpose prevention technique.

Prevention by Forbidding the Hold-and-Wait Condition
There are at least two ways to do this:

- Force a process to request all its resources in advance; it is in the blocked state until it has all resources. This is wasteful because a process must tie up all its resources from the beginning, even if it won't need them for a long time. It also can lead to starvation for processes that need several popular resources; they may never all be available at the same time. Some batch systems used this approach, however.

- Force a process to release all its resources each time it requests a new one and then re-request all resources. For example, a process that has a tape drive and a disk may also need a printer. To get the printer, it must first release the tape drive and disk. Then it requests all 3. This can also result in long waits, poor resource utilization, and the possibility of starvation.

Prevention by Forbidding the No-Preemption Condition

There are several ways to do this; two are described below.

- If a process requests a resource and it is not available, the system will preempt the resources the process currently holds. Then it must wait for all resources; not just the newly requested one.
- Let high priority processes preempt resources from low priority processes. In this case the low priority process may just be terminated.

Preemption may work if the resources being preempted have states that can be easily saved (e.g. CPU) but as a general solution, this is not effective. For example, suppose the resource being held is a data structure that requires mutual exclusion. If the data structure is preempted and given to another process, then a race condition will ensue.

Prevention by Forbidding the Circular Wait Condition

A simplistic approach is to permit a process to own only one resource at a time. This makes programming very difficult. A more common solution is based on *resource ordering*.

- Number all resource types and require processes to request resources in ascending order.
- Now, although processes may block on a resource request, it is impossible for a circular wait to develop. Consequently, there will never be deadlock.
- Proof:
    o Suppose process P_i requests resource R_n. This means that any other resource held by P_i has a number less than n.
    o Now suppose that R_n is assigned to some other process P_j.
    o P_i will block on R_n, but it cannot be deadlocked, because P_j will never request a process held by P_i. (P_j can only request resources with numbers greater than n, since it already holds R_n.)
- IBM's MVS and VAX VMS have used this approach.
- It isn't particular efficient, since it's hard to predict a standard ordering for resources and thus processes may be forced to request resources long before they are needed.
- It is also inflexible: must be built into OS; new resources require new ordering and possible modification to existing applications.
- Also, in modern applications, users don't want to have to pay attention to what resources they're using. For example, you want to open a file whenever it's appropriate, not when the proper sequence order comes up.
- Resource ordering works pretty well when semaphores control the resources being allocated. For example, the deadlock we observed in the producer consumer problem came about because semaphores were used in an incorrect order. If mutex had been assigned the highest number (i.e., it must be the last semaphore requested) the deadlock would not have occurred.

7.5 Deadlock Avoidance

Whereas deadlock prevention is a global approach that prevents deadlocks by establishing system-wide policies, deadlock avoidance avoids deadlocks by using local strategies that consider each resource request on a case-by-case basis. Notice that *both* prevention and avoidance maintain a deadlock-free system (although at a cost).

- Deadlock avoidance is based on the concept of a *safe state*, which is defined as follows: A state is safe if

- o It is not already deadlocked.
- o There is some ordering of resource allocation that will allow all active processes to complete execution without deadlocking. This is called a *safe sequence*.
- A state that is not safe is *unsafe*. This is not the same as deadlock.
- To prove that P_1... P_n is a safe sequence show that there are enough free resources for P_1 to finish. Now show that after P_1 releases its resources, P_2 will be able to acquire enough resources to finish, and that when it finishes P_3 will be able to get enough resources to finish, and so on until you show that P_n is able to finish.
- The **Banker's Algorithm** can be used to determine if a safe state exists. It is used as follows:
  - o Process requests resource.
  - o Assume request is granted; use Banker's Algorithm to determine if resulting state is safe; i.e., if a safe sequence exists.
  - o If the state is safe, then grant the resource request.
  - o Otherwise, block the process, which requested the resource until a time when the request can be granted safely.
  - o Note that when a new process is created, any initial resource requests it makes must be treated the same way.
- See example in textbook on page 228.
- Problems with Banker's Algorithm:
  - o It must be run *every* time a resource request is made.
  - o It requires processes to state maximum resource requirements in advance.

It assumes no resources will disappear from the system. For example, if a printer suddenly goes offline a currently safe state may suddenly become unsafe

7.6 Methods for Handling

- Ensure that the system will *never* enter a deadlock state.
- Allow the system to enter a deadlock state and then recover.
- Ignore the problem and pretend that deadlocks never occur in the system; used by most operating systems, including UNIX.

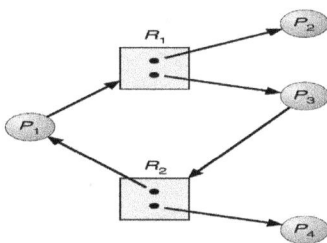

Principally, we can deal with the deadlock problem in one of three ways:

1. We can use a protocol to prevent or avoid deadlock, ensuring that the system will *never* enter a deadlock state.

2. We can allow the system to enter a deadlock state, detect it, and recover.

3. We can ignore the problem altogether, and pretend that deadlock never occur in the system.

Figure4: Resource allocation graph with a cycle but no deadlock

There are four basic approaches to deadlock management:

1. **Ignore the problem:** Most popular approach. Used in systems like UNIX.
2. **Detect and recover:** Detection algorithms require the system to maintain records of resource requests, allocations, and needs in a form the deadlock detection algorithm can readily manipulate that. The two methods outlined below are illustrations of the approach. **Resource Allocation Graphs:** -A resource graph represents the state of resource allocations and pending requests at any given time. The formal definition of the graph is given below, with an overview of how it may be used to detect deadlocks.

1. A resource allocation graph (RAG) is a directed graph {V, E}, where V is a set of vertices and E is a set of edges.

2. The set V is partitioned into two sets: P, consisting of all processes, and R, consisting of all resources. Circular vertices represent processes, square vertices represent resources.
3. If there is more than one instance of a resource type, multiple dots are placed in the resource vertex.
4. Edges from a process vertex to resource vertex (resource edge) represent pending requests for resources, edges from resource vertex to process vertex (allocation edges) represent a satisfied request.
5. It can be proven that if there are no cycles in the RAG, the system is not deadlocked. Cycle detecting algorithms are expensive: $O(N^2)$, where N = number of vertices in the graph.
6. The size of the problem can be reduced somewhat by eliminating all resource nodes from the graph. The in-edge (a request edge) and out-edge (an allocation edge) become one directed edge between two process nodes, and the resulting graph is referred to as a wait-for graph, because it shows which processes are waiting for resources, and the processes currently holding the resources
7. In a system that has multiple instances of the same resource type, cycles indicate the possibility of a deadlock, but not the certainty. Other detection methods are needed in this case.

Matrix Method

1. If a system has multiple resources of the same type (10 tape drives, 1000 i-nodes, etc.), a different approach to detection is needed. The matrix-based method described below can be used in this case.
2. Assume the system has N processes (P1, P2, ... Pn) and M resource types (R1, R2, Rm).
3. The current allocation matrix, C, is an N X M matrix where C_{ij} represents the number of instances of R_j held by P_i. In other words, each row of the matrix represents the resources held by a single process; each column represents the assignment of instances of a single resource type to processes in the system.
4. The request matrix R has entries R_{ij}, which represent the outstanding resource requests by Pj.
5. The available vector, A, is an M-dimensional vector that represents the number of instances of each resource type that are available (not allocated).
6. If a system is deadlocked, there is no way to allocate the remaining resources (represented by the available vector) so that all processes can complete.
7. The actual detection algorithm is described in the textbook. It is $O(MN^2)$, where M represents the number of resource types and N represents the number of processes.

UNIT 8

MEMORY MANAGEMENT

Introduction

The memory management subsystem is one of the most important parts of the operating system. Since the early days of computing, there has been a need for more memory than exists physically in a system. Strategies have been developed to overcome this limitation and the most successful of these is virtual memory. Virtual memory makes the system appear to have more memory than it actually has by sharing it between competing processes as they need it.

As a result of CPU scheduling, we can improve both the utilization of the CPU and the speed of the computer's response to its users. To realize this increase in performance, however, we must keep several processes in memory; that is, we must share memory. The memory management algorithms vary from a primitive bare- machine approach to paging and segmentation strategies. Each approach has its own advantages and disadvantages. Selection of a memory –management method for a specific system depends on many factors, especially on the hardware design of the system. As we shall see, many algorithms require hardware support, although recent designs have closely integrated the hardware and operating system. Memory consists of a large array of words or bytes, each with its own address. The CPU fetches instructions from memory according to the value of the program counter. These instruction may cause additional loading from and storing to specific memory address. A typical instruction – execution cycle, for example, first fetches an instruction from memory. The instruction is then decoded and may cause operands to be fetched from memory.

8.1 Address Binding

The program must be brought into memory and placed within a process for it to be executed. Depending on the memory management in use. The process may be moved between disk and memory during its execution. The collection of processes on the disk that is waiting to be brought into memory for execution forms the input queue. The normal procedure is to select one of the processes in the input queue and to load that process into memory. Classically, the binding of instructions and data to memory address can be done at any step along the way:

• Compile time: if you know at compile time where the process will reside in memory, then absolute code can be generated.

- Load time: if it is not known at compile time where the process will reside in memory, then the compiler must generate relocatable code.
- Execution time: if the process can be moved during its execution from one memory segment to another, then binding must be delayed until run time.

8.2 Logical – Versus Physical – Address Space

An address generated by the CPU is commonly referred to as a logical address, whereas an address seen by the memory unit – that is, the one loaded into the memory– address register of the memory – is commonly referred to as a physical address. The compile –time and load –time address –binding methods generate identical logical and physical addresses. However, the execution –time address binding scheme results in differing logical and physical addresses. In this case, we usually refer to the logical address as a virtual address. We use logical address and virtual address interchangeably in this text. The set of all logical addresses generated by a program is a logical-address space; the set of all physical addresses corresponding to these logical addresses is a physical – addresses space.

The run – time mapping from virtual to physical addresses is done by a hardware device called the memory – management unit (MMU). The base register is now called a relocation register. The value in the relocation register is added to every address generated by a user process at the time it is sent to memory.

8.3 Dynamic Loading

The entire program and data of a process must be in physical memory for the process to execute. The size of a process is limited to the size of physical memory. To obtain better memory – space utilization, we can use dynamic loading. With Dynamic loading, a routine is not loaded until it is called. All routines are kept On disk in a relocatable load format. The main program is loaded into memory And is executed.

8.4 Dynamic Linking and Shared Libraries

Dynamically linked libraries. Some operating systems support only static linking, in which system language libraries are treated like any other object module and are combined by the loader into the binary program image.the concept of dynamic linking is similar to that of dynamic loading. Rather then loading being postponed until execution time, linking is postponed. This feature is usually used with system libraries, such as language subroutine libraries.

This stub is a small piece of code that indicates how to locate the appropriate memory – resident library routine, or how to load the library if the routine is not already present. Thus, only programs that are compiled with the new library version are affected by the incompatible changes incorporated in it. Other programs linked before the new library was installed will continue using the older library. This system is also known as shared libraries.

8.5 Swapping

A process needs to be in memory to be executed. A process, however, can be   Swapped temporarily out of memory to a backing store, and then brought back Into memory for continued execution. For example, assume a multiprogramming environment with a round- robin CPU-scheduling algorithm. In the meantime, the CPU scheduler will allocate a time slice to some other process in memory. When each process finishes its quantum, it will be swapped with another process. A variant of this swapping policy is used for priority – based scheduling algorithms. If a higher – priority process arrives and wants service, the memory manager can swap out the lower-priority process so that it can load and execute the higher – priority process. When the higher-priority process finishes, the lower- priority process can be swapped back in and continued.

This variant of swapping is sometimes called roll out, roll in. Swapping requires a backing store. The backing store is commonly a fast disk. It Must be large enough to accommodate copies of all memory images for all users, and It must provide direct access to these memory images. The system maintains a ready queue consisting of all processes whose memory images are on the backing store or in memory and are ready to run. The context- switch time in such a swapping system is fairly high. To get an idea of the context- switch time, let us assume that the user process is of size 1 MB and the backing is a standard hard disk with a transfer rate of 5 MB per second.

8.6 Contiguous Memory allocation

The main memory must accommodate both the operating system and the various user processes. We therefore need to allocate different parts of the main memory in the most efficient way possible. This section will explain one common method, contiguous memory allocation.

The memory is usually divided into two partitions: one for the resident operating system, and one for the user processes. We may place the operating system in either low memory or high memory. The major factor affecting this decision is the location of the interrupt vector. Since the interrupt vector is often in low memory, programmers usually place the operating system in low memory as well. Thus, in this text, we shall discuss only the situation where the operating system resides in low memory.

8.7 Memory Protection

The issue of memory protection – protecting the operating system from user processes, and protecting user processes from one another.

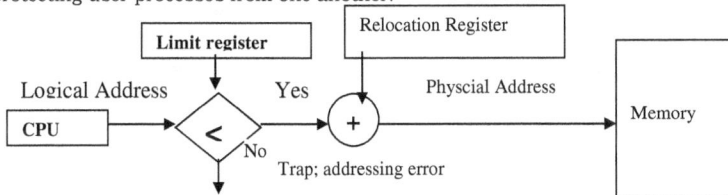

Figure: Hardware support for relocation and limit registers.

The relocation- register scheme provides an effective way to allow the operating-system size to change dynamically. This flexibility is desirable in many situations.

8.8 Memory Allocation

One of the simplest methods for memory allocations is to divide memory into several fixed – sized partitions. Each partition may contain exactly one process. Thus, the degree of multiprogramming is bound by the number of partitions. In this multiple – partition method, when a partition is free, a process is selected from the input queue and is loaded into the free partition.

As process enter the system, they are put into an input queue. The operating system takes into account the memory requirements of each process and the amount of available memory space in determining which processes are allocated memory, when a process is allocated space, it is loaded into memory and it can then compete for the CPU. When a process terminates, it releases its memory, which the operating system may then fill with another process from the input queue.

A set of holes, of various sizes, is scattered throughout memory at any given time. When a process arrives and needs memory, the system searches this set for a hole that is large enough for this process. If the hole is too large, it is split into two: one part is allocated to the arriving process; the other is returned to the set of holes. When a process terminates, it release its block of memory, which is then placed back in the set of holes. If the new hole is adjacent to other holes, these adjacent holes are merged to one large hole.

This procedure is a particular instance of the general dynamic storage allocation problem, which is how to satisfy a request of size n from a list of free holes. There are many solutions to his problem. The set of holes is searched to determine which hole is best to allocate. The first – fit,

best fit, and worst – fit strategies are the most common ones used to select a free hole from the set of available holes.
• First fit: Allocate the first hole that is big enough. Searching can start either at the beginning of the set of holes or where the previous first – fit search ended. We can stop searching as soon as we find a free hole that is large enough.
• Best fit: Allocate the smallest hole that is big enough. We must search the entire list, unless the list is kept ordered by size. This strategy produces the smallest leftover hole.
• Worst fit: Allocate the largest hole. Again, we must search the entire list, unless it is sorted by size. This strategy produces the largest leftover hole, which may be more useful than the smaller leftover hole from a best-fit approach.
Simulations have shown that both first fit and best fit are better than worst fit in Terms of decreasing both time and storage utilization. Neither first fit nor best fit. Is clearly better in terms of storage utilization, but first fit is generally faster.

8.9 Fragmentation

The overhead to keep track of this hole will be substantially larger than the hole it self. The general approach is to break the physical memory into fixed-sized blocks, and allocate memory in unit of block sizes. Which this approach, the memory allocated to a process may be slightly larger than the requested memory. The difference between these two numbers is internal fragmentation – memory that is internal to a partition but is not being used. One solution to the problem of external fragmentation is compaction. The goal is to shuffle the memory contents to place all free memory together in one large block. The simplest compaction algorithm is simply to move all processes toward one end of memory. All holes move in the order direction, producing one large hole of available memory; This scheme can be expensive.
    Another possible solution to the external – fragmentation problem is to permit the logical – address space of a process to be noncontiguous, thus allowing a process to be allocated physical memory wherever the latter is available

8.10 Paging

Paging is a memory – management scheme that permits the physical- address space of a process to be noncontiguous. Paging avoids the considerable problem of fitting the varying – sized memory chunks onto the backing store, from which most of the previous memory – management schemes suffered. When some code fragments or data residing in main memory need to be swapped out, space must be found on the backing store. The fragmentation problems discussed in connection with main memory are also prevalent with backing store, except that access is much slower, so compaction is impossible. Because of its advantages over the previous methods, paging in its various forms is commonly used in most operating systems. Traditionally, support for paging has been handled by hardware. However, recent designs have implemented paging by closely integrating the hardware and Operating system, especially on 64- bit microprocessors.

8.11 Basic Method

Physical memory is broken into fixed- sized blocks called frames. Logical memory is also broken into blocks of the same size called pages. When a process is to be executed, its pages are loaded into any available memory frames from the backing store. The backing store is divided into fixed-sized blocks that are of the same size as the memory frames.

8.12 Hardware Support

Each operating system has its own methods for storing page tables. Most allocate a page table for each process. A pointer to the page table is stored with the other register values (like the instruction counter) in the process control block. The hardware implementation of the page table can be done in several ways. In the simplest case, the page table is implemented as a set of dedicated registers. These registers should be built with very high speed logic to make the paging – address translation efficient. Every access to memory must go through the paging map, so efficiency is a major consideration. The CPU dispatcher reloads these registers, just as it reloads the other registers.

The standard solution to this problem is to use a special, small, fast- lookup hardware cache, called translation look-aside buffer (TLB). The TLB is associative, high- speed memory. Some TLB store address –space identifiers (ASID's) in each entry of the TLB. An ASID uniquely each process and is used to provide address space protection for that process. When the TLB attempts to resolve virtual page numbers, it ensures The ASID for the currently running process matches the ASID associated with the virtual page.

3.13 segmentation

A important aspect of memory management that become unavoidable with paging is the separation of the user's view of memory and the actual physical memory. The user's view of memory is not the same as actual physical memory. The user's view is mapped onto physical memory. The mapping allows differentiation between logical memory and physical memory. Segmentation are formed at program translation time by grouping together logically related items. For example, a typical process may have separate code, data, and stack segments. Data or code shared with other processes may be placed segments. Being a result of logical division, individual segments generally have different sizes. Although different segments may be placed in separate, noncontiguous area of physical memory, items belonging to a single segment must be placed in contiguous area of physical memory. Thus segmentation processes some properties of both contiguous and noncontiguous schemes for memory management.

Segmentation is quite natural for programmers who tend to think of their programs in terms of logically related entities, such as subroutines and global or local data area. A segment is essentially a collection of such entities. The segmented address space of a single process.

8.14 Basic Method

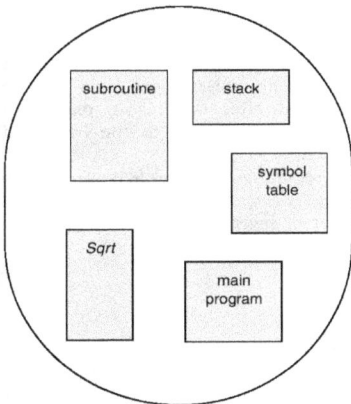

Figure : User View of a program

What is user's view of Memory? Does the user think of memory as a linear array of bytes, some containing instructions and others containing data, or is there some other preferred memory view? There is general agreement that the user or programmer of a system does not think of memory as linear array of bytes. Rather, the user prefers to view memory as a collection of variable-sized segmentation, with non necessary ordering among segments.

Segmentation is memory-management
Scheme that supports this user view of memory, A logical address space is a collection segments. Each segment has a name and a length. The address specify both the segment name and the offset within the segment. The user therefore specifies each address by two quantities: a segment name and an offset.

Logical address Space

Normally, the user program is compiled, and the compiler automatically constructs structs segments

reflecting the input program. A pascal complier might
create separate segments for (1)the global variable;
(2)the procedure call stack, to store parameters and return addresses; (3) the code portion of each or function; and (4) the local variable of each procedure and function. A FORTAN compiler might create a separate segment for each common block. Arrays might them segment numbers.

8.15 Hardware

although the user can now refer to object in the program by a two-dimensional address, the actual physical memory is still, of course, a one-dimensional sequence of bytes. Thus, we must define an implementation to map two dimensional user-define addresses into one-dimensional physical address. This mapping is effected by a *segment table*. Each entry of the segment table

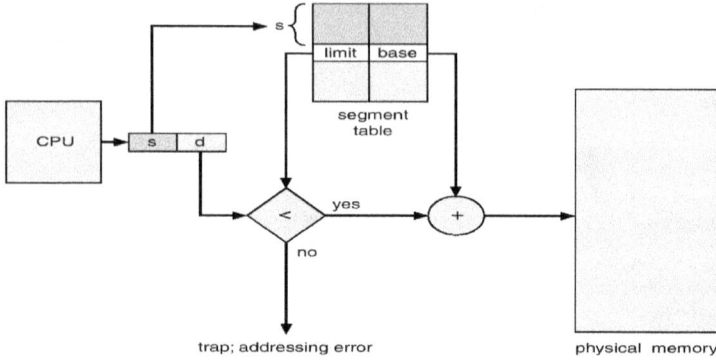

has a segment *base* and a segment *limit* The segment base contains the starting physical address where the segment resides in memory, whereas the segmentation limit specifies the length of the segment.

Figure: Segmentation hardware

A logical address consists of two parts: a segmentation number, s, and an offset into that segment, d. The segment number is used as an index into the segment table .The offset d of the logical address must be between 0 and the segment limit.

8.16 Implementation of Segment Tables

Segmentation is closely related to the partition model management presented earlier, the main difference being that one program may consist of several segments. Segmentation is a more complex concept, however, which is why we are describing it after discussing paging. A segmentation table kept in registers can be referenced quickly the addition to the base and comparison with the limit can be done simultaneously to save time.
In the case where a 0rogram may consist of a large number of segments, it is not feasible to keep the segment table in registers, so we must keep it in memory. A *Segment-table base registered* (STBR) points to the segment table. Also, because the number of segments used by a program may vary widely, a *segment-table length registered* (STLR) is used.

8.17 Segmentation with paging

Both paging and segmentation have their advantages and disadvantages. In fact, of the two most popular microprocessors now being used, the Motorola6800 line is designed on a flat address space, whereas the Intel 80×86 family is based on segmentation. Both are merging memory models toward a mixture of paging and Segmentation. It is possible to combine these two schemes to improve on each. This combination is best illustrated by two different architectures-the innovative but not widely used MULTICS system and the Intel 386.

8.18 MULTICS

In the MULTICS system, a logical address is formed from an 18-bit segment number and a 16-bit offset. Although this scheme create a 34-bit address space, the segment-table entries as we have segments, as there need not be empty segment-table entries.
However, with segment of 64K words, each of which consists of 36 bits, the average segment size could be large and external fragmentation is not a problem, the search time to allocate a segment, using first-fit, could be long. Thus, we may waste memory due to external fragmentation, or waste time due to lengthy searches, or both.

The solution adopted was to *page* the *Segments*. Paging eliminates external fragmentation and make the allocation problem trivial: any empty frame can be used for a desired page. Each page in MULTICS consists of 1K words. Thus, the segment offset is broken into a 6-bit page number and a 10-bit page offset. The frame number is combined with the page offset to form a physical address.

8.19 OS/2 32-Bit Version

The IBM OS/2 32-bit version is an operating system running on top of the Intel 386 architecture. The 386 uses segmentation with paging for memory management. The maximum number of segments per process is 16K, and each segment can be as large as 4 gigabytes. The page size is 4K bytes. The logically address space of a process is divided into two partitions. The first partition consists of up to 8K segmentation that are private to that process. The second partition consists of up to 8K segments that are shared among all the processes. Information about first partition is kept in the *logical description table* (LDT), information about the second partition is kept in the *global description table* (GDT). Each entry in the LDT and GDT table consist of 8 bytes, with detailed information about a particular segment including the base location and length of that segment.

The logical address is a pair, where the selector is a 16-bit number:

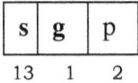

s	g	p
13	1	2

in which *s* designates the segment number, *g* indicates whether the segment is in the GDT or LDT, and *p* deals with protection. The offset is a 32-bit number specifying the location of the byte within segment in question.

The machine has six segment registers, allowing six segments to be addressed at any one by a process. It has six 8-byte micro program registered to hold the corresponding description from either the LDT or GDT.

UNIT 9

FILE SYSTEM INTERFACE

9.1 File concept

Another key aspect of any operating system is the concept of a file. A file is nothing more than a related set of bytes on disk or other media. These bytes are labeled with a name, which is then used as a means of referring to that set of bytes. In most cases, it is through the name that the operating system is able to track down the file's exact location on the disk. _File_ is a named collection of information The file manager administers the collection by:

- Storing the information a device , Mapping the block storage to the logical view , Allocating/de-allocating storage, Providing file directories.

- A file system provides the mechanism for on-line storage of and access to information belonging to the OS and its users. Here, we first discuss the file system in very general terms and then explain how it is implemented in Nachos. Note that this is not an exhaustive discussion of a file system; it is rather an overview providing information sufficient for you to understand the Nachos file system.

- The logical storage unit for information is _files_. These are mapped by the OS into physical devices. In general, they are treated as a sequence of bits, bytes, lines or records - the meaning is defined by the file's creator. Information about all the files is kept in a directory structure that resides on secondary storage along with the files.

The interface that the OS provides for the file system comprises, among other things, of operations to manipulate files, e.g., creating, opening, writing or truncating a file. Many of these file operations involving searching the directory structure for the entry associated with the file. Since searching the file entry for each operation performed on the file can be expensive, the OS maintains a small table containing information about all open files (_the open-file table_). When a file operation is requested, an index into this file table is used to get the appropriate entry. When the file is no longer being used, it is closed by the process and the operating system removes its entry from the open file table. Each process also maintains a table of all the files that it has opened. This stores information about how the file(s) are being used, e.g., the current location of the file pointer. Each entry in this table points to the corresponding entry in the open-file table.

9.2 **File Attribute**

A file is named, for the c1onvenience of its human users, and is referred to its users, and is referred to by its name. the file's owner might another might write the file toa floppy disk or magnetic tape, and might read it of onto another system.

A file has certain other attributes, which vary from one operating system to another, but typically consist of these:

• Name: the symbolic file name is the only information kept in human readable form.

• Type: this information is needed for those systems that support different types.

• Location: this information is a pointer to a device and to the location of the file on that device.

• Size: the current size of the file (in bytes, word or blocks), and possibly the maximum allocated size are included in this attribute.

• Protection: Access-control information controls who can do reading, writing, executing, soon.

• Time, date and user identification: information may be kept for creation, last modification, and last use.

9.3 **File operations**

• **Creating a file**: Two steps are necessary to create a file. First, space in the file system must be found for the file. The directory entry records the name of the file and the location in the file system, and possibly other information.

• **Writing a file:** To write a file, we make a system call specifying both the name of the file and the information to be written to the file. Given the name of the file, the system searches the directory to find the location of the file. The system must keep a write pointer to the location in the file where the next write is to take place. The write pointer must be updated whenever a write occurs.

• **Reading a file:** To read from a file, we use a system call that specifies the name of the file and where (in memory) the next block of the file should be put. Again, the directory is searched for the associated directory entry, and the system needs to keep a read pointer to the location in the file where the next read is to take place. Once the read has taken place, the read pointer is updated. A given process is usually only reading or writing a given file, and the current operations location is kept as a per – process current – file – position pointer. Both the read and write operations use this same pointer, saving space and reducing the system complexity.

• **Reposition within a file:** The directory is searched for the appropriate entry, and the current-file-position is set to a given value. Repositioning within a file does not need to involve any actual I/O. This file operation is also known as a file seek.

• **Deleting a file:** To delete a file, we search the directory for the named file. Having found the associated directory entry, we release all file space, so that it can be reused by other files, and erase the directory entry.

• **Truncating a file:** the user may want to erase the contents of a file but keep its attributes. Rather forcing the user to delete the file and then recreate it, this function allows all attributes to remain unchanged – except for file length –but lets the file be reset to length zero and its file space released.

9.4 Access Methods

File store information. When it is used, this information must be accessed and read into computer memory. The information in the file can be accessed in several ways. Some systems provide only one access method for files. Other systems, such as those of IBM, support many access methods, and choosing the right one for a particular application is a major design problem.

9.4.1 Sequential Access

The simplest access method is sequential access. Information in the file is processed in order, one record after the other. This mode of access is by far the most common for example, editors and compilers usually access files in this fashion.

9.4.2 Direct Access

Another method is direct access. A file is made up of fixed length of logical records that allow programs to read and write records rapidly in no particular order. The direct access method is based on a disk model of a file. A direct access, the file is viewed as a numbered sequence of blocks or records. A direct access file allow arbitrator block to read or write.

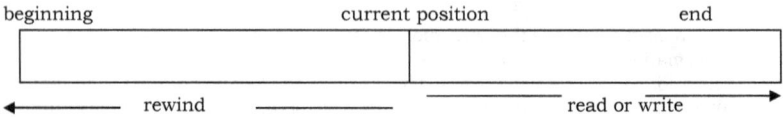

Direct access file are of great use for immediate access to large amounts of information. Database are often of this type. When a query concerning a particular subject arrives. The file operation must modified to include the block number as a parameter.

9.4.3 Other Access Methods

Other access method generally can be built on top of a direct-access method. These additional methods generally involve the construction of an index for the file. The index, like an index in the back of a book, contains pointer to the various blocks. To find an entry in the file, we first search the index, and then use the pointer to access the file directly and to find the desired entry. With large files, the index file itself may become too large to be kept in memory. One solution is to create an index file. The primary index file would contain pointer to secondary index files, which would point to the actual data items.

9.5 Directory Structure

The file systems of computers can be extensive. Some systems store thousands of files on hundreds of gigabytes of disk. To manage all these data, we need to organize them. This organization is usually done in two parts. First, the file system is broken into *partitions,* also known as *minidisks* in the IBM world or volumes in the PC and Macintosh arenas. A set of logically associated files and sub directories. File manager provides set of controls:

- enumerate
- copy
- rename
- delete
- traverse
- etc.

Typically, each disk on a system contains at least one partition, which is a low-level structure in which files and directories reside. Sometimes, partitions are used to provide several separate areas within one disk, each treated as a separate storage device, whereas other systems allow partitions to be larger than a disk to group disks into one logical structure. In this way, the user needs to be concerned with only the logical directory and file structure, and can ignore completely the problems of physically allocating space for files. For this reason partitions can be thought of as virtual disks.

- **Search for a file.** We need to be able to search a directory structure to find the entry for a particular file. Since files have symbolic names and similar names may indicate a relationship between files, we may want to be able to find all files whose names match a particular pattern.
- **Create a file.** New files need to be created and added to the directory.
- **Delete a file.** When a file is no longer needed, we want to remove it from the directory.
- **List a directory.** We need to be able to list the files in a directory, and the contents of the directory entry for each file in the list.
- **Rename a file.** Because the name of a file represents its contents to its users, the name must be changeable when the contents or use of the file changes. Renaming a file may also allow its position within the directory structure to be changed.

• **Traverse the file system.** It is useful to be able to access every directory, and every file within a directory structure.

For reliability, it is a good idea to save the contents and structure of the entire file system at regular intervals. This saving often consists of copying all files to magnetic tape. This technique provides a backup copy in case of system failure or if the file is simply no longer in use. In this case, the file can be copied to tape, and the disk space of that file released for issue by another file.

9.5.1 Single-level Directory

A single-level directory has significant limitations, however, when the number of files increases or when there is more than one user. Since all files are in the same directory, they must have unique names. If we have two users who call their data file test, then the unique-name rule is violated. (For example, in one programming class, 23 students called the program for their second assignment prog2; another 11 called it assing2.) Although file names are generally selected to reflect the content of the file, they are often limited I length. The MS-DOS operating system allows only 11-character file names; UNIX allows 255 characters.

Two-level Directory

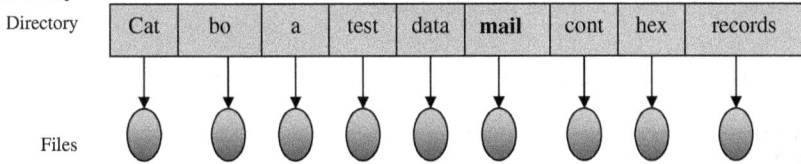

Directory

| Cat | bo | a | test | data | **mail** | cont | hex | records |

Files

9.5.2 Two level directory

In the two-level directory structure, each user has her own user file directory (UFD). Each UFD has a similar structure, but lists only the files of a single user. When a user job starts or a user logs in, the system's master file directory (MFD) is searched. The master file directory is indexed by user name or account number, and each entry points to the UFD for that user.

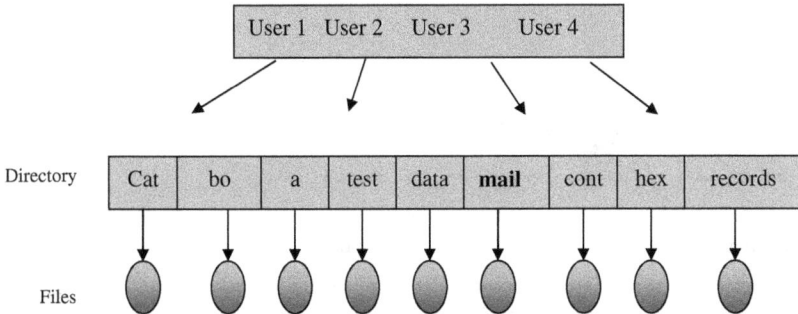

User 1   User 2   User 3   User 4

Directory

| Cat | bo | a | test | data | **mail** | cont | hex | records |

Files

9.5.3 Tree-Structured Directories

Once we have seen how to view a two-level directory as a two-level tree, the natural generalization is to extend the directory structure to a tree of arbitrary height. This generalization allows users to create their own sub-directories and to organize their files accordingly. The MS-DOS system, for instance, is structured as a tree. In fact, a tree is the most common directory structure. The tree has a root directory. Every file in the system has a unique path name. A path name is the path from the root, through all the subdirectories, to a specified file.

9.5.4 Acyclic-Graph Directories
Consider two programmers who are working on a joint project. The files associated with that project can be stored in a subdirectory, separating them from other projects and files of the two programmers. But since both programmers are equally responsible for the project, both want the subdirectory to be in their own directories. The common subdirectory should be shared.

A shared directory or file will exist in the file system in two (or more) places at once. Notice that a shared file (or directory is not the same as two copies of the file. With two copies, each programmer can view the copy rather than the original, but if one programmer changes the file, the changes will not appear in the other's copy. With a shared file, there is only one actual file, so any changes made by one person would be immediately visible to the other. This form of sharing is particularly important for share subdirectories; a new file created by one person will automatically appear in all the shared subdirectories.

9.6 File-System Mounting

A file must be opened before it is used, a file system must be mounted before it can be available to processes on the system. More specifically, the directory structure can be built out of multiple partitions, which must be mounted to make them available within the file system name space.

The mount procedure is straightforward. The operating system is given the name or the device, and the location within the file structure at which to attach the file system(or mount point). Typically, a mount is an point is an empty directory at which the mounted file system will be attached. For instance, on a UNIX system, a file system containing user's home directory name with /home, as in /home/Jane. Mounting that file system would result in the path name/user/Jane to reach the same directory.

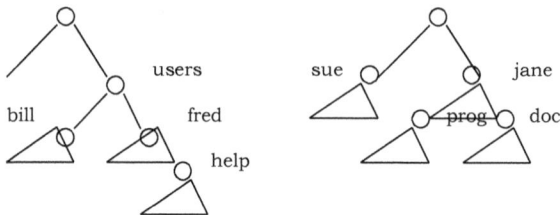

(a) Existing   (b) Unmounted partition

where the triangles represent sub trees of directories that are of interest. In an existing file system, an Unmounted partition residing on /device/disk over /users are shown.
Systems impose semantics to clarify functionality. For example. A system may disallow a mount over a directory and obscure the directory's existing files until the file system is Unmounted, terminating the use of the file system and allowing access to the original files in that directory. An another example, a system may allow the same file system to be mounted repeatedly, at different mount points.

9.7 File Sharing

The motivation for file sharing and some of the difficulties involved in allowing users to share files. Such file sharing is very desirable for users who want to collaborated and to reduce the effort required to achieve a computing goal. user-oriented operating system must accommodate the need to share files in spite of the inherit difficulties.

9.8 Multiple Users

When an operating system accommodates multiple users the issue of tile sharing ,file naming, and file protection become preeminent. Given a directory structure. That allows file to be shared by users, the system must mediate the file sharing. The system either can allow a user to access to the files.
To implement sharing and protection, the system must maintain more file and directory attributes than on a single user system. Although there have been many approaches to this topic historically most systems have evolved to the concept of file/directory owner and group.

9.9 Remote File Systems

The advent of keyword allowed communication between remote computers. Networking allows the sharing of resources spread within a campus or even around the world. Through the evolution of network and file technology, file-sharing methods have changed. In the first implemented method, users manually transfer files between machines.

9.10 Protection

When information is kept in a computer system, a major concern is its protection from both physical damage and improper access. Reliability is generally provided by duplicate copies of files. Many computer-operator copy disk file it tape at regular intervals to maintain a copy should a file system be accidentally destroy.
 Protection can be provided in many ways. For a small single user system, we might provide protection by physically removing the floppy disk and locking them in a desk or file cabinet. In a multi-user system, however, other mechanism are needed.

50

UNIT 10

SECURITY

10.1   The Security Problem
10.2   User Authentication
10.3   Program Threats
10.4   System Threats
10.5   Securing Systems and Facilities
10.6   Intrusion Detection
10.7   Cryptography
10.8   Computer-Security
10.9   Classifications

10.1 The Security Problem

• Critical national infrastructure is now online
• Corporate data, financial data is now connected
• "However, the nature of the internet demands at the very least daily scans of Usenet posts, E-mail lists, and Web sites for information on security breaches and the availability of patches" – eWeek, 1996

10.2 User Authentication

Basic authentication is a standard which nearly all browsers support. When you access a site and you see a standard popup window which asks for your username and password, your are using basic authentication. An example from Internet Explorer can be found below

10.3 Program Threats

Logic bomb
Hidden program activated under certain conditions
Ex: if lookup of "Bill Ellison" in payroll file fails then for every entry in payroll file if entry.salary > 100K then set entry.salary = 10K endif endfor endif

Back door

> Hole in system security deliberately installed by designers or maintainers Intent not always sinister

Trojan Horse
> Code segment that misuses its environment.
> Exploits mechanisms for allowing programs written by users to be executed by other users.

Trap Door
> Specific user identifier or password that circumvents normal security procedures.
> Could be included in a compiler.

10.4 System Threats

• Worms - use spawn mechanism; standalone program.
• Internet worm
  o Exploited UNIX networking features (remote access) and bugs in *finger* and *sendmail* programs.
  o Grappling hook program uploaded main worm program.

- Viruses - fragment of code embedded in a legitimate program.
- Mainly effect microcomputer systems.
- Downloading viral programs from public bulletin boards or exchanging floppy disks containing an infection.

10.5 Securing Systems and Facilities

The problem of system security starts with discovering the identity of the user on the other end of the communications link. In this article, Joseph Sinclair discusses three familiar approaches for identifying users, highlights their strengths and weaknesses (alone and in combinations), and provides some examples of each.

Computer security is the generic name for collection of tools designed to protect data and to thwart off hackers.

- Secrecy — Prevent/detect/deter improper disclosure of information
- Integrity — Prevent/detect/deter improper modification of information
- Availability — Prevent/detect/deter improper denial of access to services provided by the system
- Note the improper use rather than unauthorized
- Authorized users are accountable for their actions.

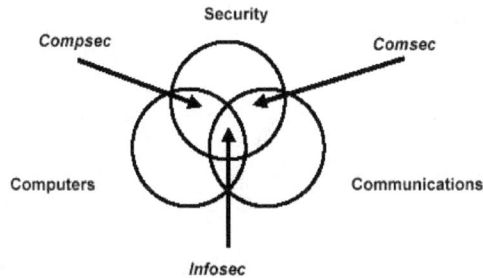

10.6 Intrusion Detection

Simply put, an **intrusion** is someone attempting to break into or misuse your system. How you define *someone* and *break into* or *misuse* is up to you. Let us assume that you know what you wouldn't like to see someone do on your system (for more information, see the section on security policy).

An IDS may also perform its own system monitoring. It may keep aggregate statistics which give a system usage profile. These statistics can be derived from a variety of sources such as CPU usage, disk I/O, memory usage, activities by users, number of attempted logins, etc. These statistics must be continually updated to reflect the current system state. They are correlated with an internal model which will allow the IDS to determine if a series of actions constitute a potential intrusion. This model may describe a set of intrusion scenarios or possibly encode the profile of a clean system.

Characteristics of a Good Intrusion Detection System

An intrusion detection system should address the following issues, regardless of what mechanism it is based on:

1. It must **run continually** without human supervision. The system must be reliable enough to allow it to run in the background of the system being observed. However, it should not be a "black box". That is, its internal workings should be examinable from outside.
2. It must be **fault tolerant** in the sense that it must survive a system crash and not have its knowledge-base rebuilt at restart.

3. On a similar note to above, it must **resist subversion**. The system can monitor itself to ensure that it has not been subverted.
4. It must impose **minimal overhead** on the system. A system that slows a computer to a crawl will simply not be used.
5. It must **observe deviations** from normal behavior.
6. It must be **easily tailored** to the system in question. Every system has a different usage pattern, and the defense mechanism should adapt easily to these patterns.
7. It must cope with **changing system behavior** over time as new applications are being added. The system profile will change over time, and the IDS must be able to adapt.
8. Finally, it must be **difficult to fool**.

The last point raises an issue about the type of errors likely to occur in the system. These can be neatly categorized as either **false positive, false negative**, or **subversion** errors. A false positive occurs when the system classifies an action as anomalous (a possible intrusion) when it is a legitimate action. A false negative occurs when an actual intrusive action has occurred but the system allows it to pass as non-intrusive behavior. A subversion error occurs when an intruder modifies the operation of the intrusion detector to force false negatives to occur.

False positive errors will lead users of the intrusion detection system to ignore its output, as it will classify legitimate actions as intrusions. The occurrences of this type of error should be minimized (it may not be possible to completely eliminate them) so as to provide useful information to the operators. If too many false positives are generated, the operators will come to ignore the output of the system over time, which may lead to an actual intrusion being detected but ignored by the users.

A false negative error occurs when an action proceeds even though it is an intrusion. False negative errors are more serious than false positive errors because they give a misleading sense of security. By allowing all actions to proceed, a suspicious action will not be brought to the attention of the operator. The intrusion detection system is now a liability as the security of the system is less than it was before the intrusion detector was installed.

Subversion errors are more complex and tie in with false negative errors. An intruder could use knowledge about the internals of an intrusion detection system to alter its operation, possibly allowing anomalous behavior to proceed. The intruder could then violate the system's operational security constraints. This may be discovered by a human operator examining the logs from the intrusion detector, but it would appear that the intrusion detection system still *seems* to be working correctly.

Another form of subversion error is fooling the system over time. As the detection system is observing behavior on the system over time, it may be possible to carry out operations each of which when taken individually pose no threat, but taken as an aggregate form a threat to system integrity. How would this happen? As mentioned previously, the detection system is continually updating its notion of normal system usage. As time goes by a change in system usage patterns is expected, and the detection system must cope with this. But if an intruder could perform actions over time which were just slightly outside of normal system usage, then it is possible that the actions could be accepted as legitimate where as they really form part of an intrusion attempt. The detection system would have come to accept each of the individual actions as slightly suspicious, but not a threat to the system. What it would not realize is that the combination of these actions would form a serious threat to the system.

10.7 Cryptography

Give the best or shortest possible word to describe the following terms:
a. Cryptography –The practice (or art) of using encryption to conceal text
b. Cryptology – The art of hidden writing
c. Cryptographer –Invents encryption algorithms ("Good Guys")
d. Cryptanalyst – Attempts to break encryption algorithms ("Bad Guys")
e. Cryptosystem –A system for encryption and decryption
f. Cipher text –A message in the encrypted form
g. Plain text / clear text – A message in its original form

h. Encryption – The process of coding a message such that its meaning is concealed
i. Decryption –The process of transforming an encrypted message into the original form

The encryption algorithm and decryption algorithm uses one single key for both ciphering and deciphering. Enciphering the plaintext yields the cipher text. Only the cipher text is transmitted over the insecure channel. Deciphering of the cipher text yields the original message. The shared key has to be transported via a secure channel

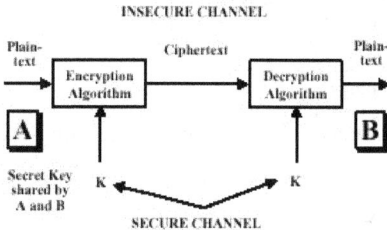

Name four avenues where cryptanalysis can be performed.
- Cipher text Only – Cryptanalyst only knows cipher text
- Known Plaintext – Cryptanalyst knows some plaintext-cipher text pairs
- Chosen Plaintext – Cryptanalyst knows some plaintext-cipher text pairs for plaintext of the cryptanalyst's choice
- Chosen Cipher text – Cryptanalyst knows some plaintext-cipher text pairs for cipher text of the cryptanalyst's choice

Name the 3 Basic Encryption techniques.
- Substitution
- Permutation (or transposition)
- Combinations and iterations of these

10.8 Computer-Security

Introduction to Computer Security" goes far beyond just describing the basic ABC's of security. The course outlines the problems and shortfalls of today's common security practices. Students uncover the reasons that problems exist in their security configuration or systems and services. This gives students the awareness needed to discover and/or prevent similar problems and to identify the situations that breed them. Of course, we also convey a list of many common vulnerabilities and how to fix them.
Companies whose employees complete this course are one step ahead of their competition. They are in a better position to protect their proprietary data. Also, they can avoid the time and service loss associated with an attackSome examples of security violations that are governed by these policies are:

A. Bandwidth over subscription
B. Virus infections
C. Attacks against another system
D. Attacks against a mission critical system that requires special circumstances for service disconnection.
E. Dormant compromised system (confirmed to be compromised but not currently being used in a malicious manner)
F. Stolen IP Address
G. Denial of Service Attacks
H. Copyright violation
I. Unauthorized scanning of ports
J. Second offense of the same type incident
K. Active compromised system

10.9 Classifications

- **alert** Advisories on various security vulnerabilities
- **dict** Dictionaries and word lists
- **doc** Security related documents
  - **access_control** Documents related to access control
  - **alert** Security advisories, security bulletins, patches, fixes, etc.
  - **authentication** Documents related to authentication
  - **books+reviews** Blurbs about security books, and reviews of books and software
  - **commercials** Documents that describe commercial packages
  - **cryptology** Documents related to cryptology
  - **email** Documents related to security and e-mail, privacy enhancement, etc.
  - **equipment** Documents that contain information relevant to security related equipment
  - **evaluation** Documents that contain information relevant to the evaluation of the security aspects of systems
  - **faq** Documents that contains answers to Frequently Asked Questions (FAQs)
  - **firewalls** Documents related to Firewalls
  - **forensics** Documents related to software forensics
  - **general** Documents regarding the general aspects of security
  - **genetic_algorithms** Documents regarding genetic algorithms
  - **guidelines** Guidelines on how to keep your system secure (or securer)
  - **institutional_policies** Documents related to policies on various kinds of institutions.
  - **intrusion_detection** Documents on intrusion detection
  - **law+ethics** Documents on computer security and the law, and computer use/abuse and ethics.
  - **maintenance** Documents on software maintenance
  - **misc** Documents that don't fit anywhere else
  - **morris_worm** Papers about Robert T.'s 1988 escapade.
  - **network** Documents on network security
  - **passwords** Documents on password security
  - **policy** Documents on security policy
  - **privacy** Documents on privacy
  - **rfc** RFC indexes, information about RFCs and information on how to retrieve them.
  - **risk** Documents on risk on computers
  - **social** Documents on the social aspects of security and privacy
  - **standards** Standards and documents about standards
  - **tech_tips** Tech tips
  - **tools** Documents about various security tools
  - **true_stories** True Stories regarding security and privacy issues
  - **trusted_systems** Documents about trusted systems
  - **viruses+alife** Documents about viruses, anti-viruses and artificial life
- **news+lists** Security newsgroups and mailing lists
- **patches** Bug-fixes that mend security holes on various systems
- **tools** Software tools
  - **amiga** Tools for Amiga systems
    - **privacy/cryptology** Tools for enciphering documents, breaking ciphers, creating digital signatures, etc.
    - **maintenance** System maintenance
    - **viruses** Virus detectors and related tools.
    - **tripwires** Tools for installing tripwires in systems
    - **misc** Tools that don't fit anywhere else
    - **dos** Tools for DOS/PC
  - **access_control** Tools related to access control
  - **authentication** User authentication and verification
  - **privacy/cryptology** Tools for enciphering documents, breaking ciphers, creating digital signatures, etc.
  - **firewalls** Firewalls and firewall related tools and utilities
  - **maintenance** System maintenance

o **networking** Network management tools, network browsers, network analyzers, network tools, etc.

56

UNIT 11

UNIX

11.1 Introduction to UNIX

UNIX is an *operating system*. The job of an operating system is to orchestrate the various parts of the computer -- the processor, the on-board memory, the disk drives, keyboards, video monitors, etc. -- to perform useful tasks. The operating system is the master controller of the computer, the glue that holds together all the components of the system, including the administrators, programmers, and users. When you want the computer to do something for you, like start a program, copy a file, or display the contents of a directory, it is the operating system that must perform those tasks for you.

More than anything else, the operating system gives the computer its recognizable characteristics. It would be difficult to distinguish between two completely different computers, if they were running the same operating system. Conversely, two identical computers, running different operating systems, would appear completely different to the user.

UNIX was created in the late 1960s, in an effort to provide a multiuser, multitasking system for use by programmers. The philosophy behind the design of UNIX was to provide simple, yet powerful utilities that could be pieced together in a flexible manner to perform a wide variety of tasks.

The UNIX operating system comprises three parts: The kernel, the standard utility programs, and the system configuration files.

Accessing a UNIX System

There are many ways that you can access a UNIX system. The main mode of access to a UNIX machine is through a *terminal*, which usually includes a keyboard, and a video monitor. For each terminal connected to the UNIX system, the kernel runs a process called a *tty* that accepts input from the terminal, and sends output to the terminal. Tty processes are general programs, and must be told the capabilities of the terminal in order to correctly read from, and write to, the terminal. If the tty process receives incorrect information about the terminal type, unexpected results can occur.

Console

Every UNIX system has a main console that is connected directly to the machine. The console is a special type of terminal that is recognized when the system is started. Some UNIX system operations must be performed at the console. Typically, the console is only accessible by the system operators, and administrators.

Dumb terminals

Some terminals are referred to as "dumb" terminals because they have only the minimum amount of power required to send characters as input to the UNIX system, and receive characters as output from the UNIX system.

Personal computers are often used to emulate dumb terminals, so that they can be connected to a UNIX system.

Dumb terminals can be connected directly to a UNIX machine, or may be connected remotely, through a modem or a terminal server.

Smart terminals

Smart terminals, like the X terminal, can interact with the UNIX system at a higher level. Smart terminals have enough on-board memory and processing power to support graphical interfaces. The interaction between a smart terminal and a UNIX system can go beyond simple characters to include icons, windows, menus, and mouse actions.

The UNIX File System

Most UNIX machines store their files on magnetic disk drives. A disk drive is a device that can store information by making electrical imprints on a magnetic surface. One or more heads skim close to the spinning magnetic plate, and can detect, or change, the magnetic state of a given spot on the disk. The drives use disk controllers to position the head at the correct place at the correct time to read from, or write to, the magnetic surface of the plate. It is often possible to partition a single disk drive into more than one logical storage area. This section describes how the UNIX operating system deals with a raw storage device like a disk drive, and how it manages to make organized use of the space.

How the UNIX file system works

Every item in a UNIX file system can be defined as belonging to one of four possible types:
Ordinary files

> Ordinary files can contain text, data, or program information. An ordinary file cannot contain another file, or directory. An ordinary file can be thought of as a one-dimensional array of bytes.

Directories

> In a previous section, we described directories as containers that can hold files, and other directories. A directory is actually implemented as a file that has one line for each item contained within the directory. Each line in a directory file contains only the name of the item, and a numerical reference to the location of the item. The reference is called an *i-number*, and is an index to a table known as the *i-list*. The i-list is a complete list of all the storage space available to the file system.

Special files

> Special files represent input/output (i/o) devices, like a tty (terminal), a disk drive, or a printer. Because UNIX treats such devices as files, a degree of compatibility can be achieved between device i/o, and ordinary file i/o, allowing for the more efficient use of software. Special files can be either *character special files,* that deal with streams of characters, or *block special files*, that operate on larger blocks of data. Typical block sizes are 512 bytes, 1024 bytes, and 2048 bytes.

Links

> A link is a pointer to another file. Remember that a directory is nothing more than a list of the names and i-numbers of files. A directory entry can be a *hard link*, in which the i-number points directly to another file. A hard link to a file is indistinguishable from the file itself. When a hard link is made, then the i-numbers of two different directory file entries point to the same node. For that reason, hard links cannot span across file systems. A *soft link* (or *symbolic link*) provides an indirect pointer to a file. A soft link is implemented as a directory file entry containing a pathname. Soft links are distinguishable from files, and can span across file systems. Not all versions of UNIX support soft links.

A brief tour of the UNIX filesystem

The actual locations and names of certain system configuration files will differ under different implementations of UNIX. Here are some examples of important files and directories under version 9 of the HP-UX operating system:

/hp-ux
> The kernel program

/dev/
> Where special files are kept

/bin/
> Executable system utilities, like sh, cp, rm

/etc/
> System configuration files and databases

/lib/
> Operating system and programming libraries

/tmp/
> System scratch files (all users can write here)

/lost+found/
> Where the file system checker puts detached files

/usr/bin/
    Additional user commands
/usr/include/
    Standard system header files
/usr/lib/
    More programming and system call libraries
/usr/local/
    Typically a place where local utilities go
/usr/man
    The manual pages are kept here

11.2 A Sample Login Session

The School of Oceanography has several Unix workstations available for use in two public workrooms, 265 MSB and 212 ORB (more information). Any of these accept logins over the campus network as well. Our principal server is tsunami.ocean whose environment is mirrored on reef, shoal, dune and jetty.

11.2.1 Logging On

When you first connect to one of the Unix computers you will see the prompt:

    login:

If you see only the prompt Password: you probably used rlogin. rlogin assumes that your username is the same on all computers and enters it for you. If your username is different, don't worry, just press <CR> until you see the login: prompt and start from scratch.

At the login: prompt, type in your username. *Be careful to type only lowercase!* The Unix operating system is ``case sensitive.'' If you type your username in mixed case (Rarmour rather than rarmour, for example) the computer will not recognize it.

Your Password

Once you have typed in your username you will be prompted to type in your password. Type carefully! It won't be displayed on the screen.

When you first login, you should change your password with the yppasswd command. Remember again-these are lower case commands and Unix insists that you type them that way.

Your password should be longer than six characters. It's a good idea to make it mixed case or to stick some numbers or symbols in it, like ``,'' or ``^''. One of few password restrictions is that the password cannot be all-numeric (like 5534553). Because of a bug on the Sun computers, do not put a ``:'' in your password.

In the interests of self-preservation, *don't* set your password to your username, to ``password'' or to any information which people are likely to know about you (your real name, your nickname, your pet dog's name).

If you mistype your username or password you will get a suspicious message from the computer and see the login: prompt again.

The motd

If you type your username and password correctly, the computer will begin running the login program. It starts by displaying a special ``message of the day''---contained in the /etc/motd file. This file will usually contain information about the computer you are logging onto, maybe a basic message about getting help, and any important system messages from the system manager.

Initialization Files

When you log in the Unix login program finally starts up a command ``shell.'' Users do not deal with the operating system directly. Instead they interact with a shell, which is initialized with several pieces of information (such as your username, login directory and ``path''). By default all users use the C shell (the program /bin/csh) and interact with it.

There are a couple of files read by this shell when your login session starts up. These are the .cshrc file and the .login file. These files are created when your account is created. As you learn more about how Unix and the C shell work, you may want to customize these files.

If your files get corrupted for some reason, copies of the system defaults are available in /usr/local/skel/.

Using the System

Finally you are logged in! You will see a prompt like one of the following three:

    pooh>

    {coil: 1}

    %

just waiting for you to type something. Throughout the Unix Tutorial section we will use % to indicate the computer's ``ready'' prompt.

ls

Okay, let's try a simple command. Type ls and press enter. Ls is the program to list files in a directory. Right now you may or may not see any files-not seeing any files doesn't mean you don't have any! Just plain ls won't list hidden files (files whose names start with ``.'', like .login). Now try typing:

    %ls -a

Don't actually type the % symbol! Remember, that's the computer's prompt which indicates it is ready to accept input. The spacing should be exactly as shown. ls followed by a space, followed by a -a. The -a is a ``flag'' which tells the ls program to list all files.

For more about command flags see below.

cd

Just for fun, let's look at the contents of another directory, one with lots of files. Directory names in Unix are straightforward. They are all arranged in a tree structure from the root directory ``/''.

For now, use cd to change your directory to the /bin directory. Type:

    % cd /bin

and press <CR>. Now type ls again. You should see a long list of files-in fact, if you look carefully you will see files with the names of the commands we've been typing (like ls and cd). Note that the /bin in the command we typed above was *not* a flag to cd. It was a ``parameter.'' Flags tell commands how to act, parameters tell them what to act on.

Now return to your login directory with:

    % cd

Entering cd with no parameter returns you to your home directory. You can check to make sure that it worked by entering:

% pwd

which prints your current (or ``working'') directory. The computer should return a line of words separated by ``/'' symbols which should look something like:

/home/*username*

Whatever it returns, the list should end in your username.

11.2.2 Using the On-line Man Pages

Most Unix commands have very short and sometimes cryptic names like ls. This can make remembering them difficult. Fortunately there are on-line manual pages which allow you to display information on a specific program (to list all the flags of ls, for example) or list all the information available on a certain topic.

man

To investigate other flags to the ls command (such as which flags will display file size and ownership) you would type man ls.

man -k

The second way of using the on-line manual pages is with man -k. In this case you use a word you expect to be in a one-line description of the command you wish to find. To find a program which ``lists directory contents'' you might type man -k dir. Partial words can be used and this is one of the few places in Unix where upper and lower case are allowed to match each other.

11.2.3 Using man and more

Try it now. Use man ls to find out how to make the ls program print the sizes of your files as well as their names. After typing man ls and pressing , note how man displays a screenful of text and then waits with a prompt --More-- at the bottom of the screen.

What man is doing is sending everything it wants to display to the screen through a program known as a ``pager'' The pager program is called more. When you see --More-- (in inverse video) at the bottom of the screen, just press the space-bar to see the next screenful. Press <CR> to scroll a line at a time.

Have you found the flag yet? The -s flag should display the size in kilobytes. You don't need to continue paging once you have found the information you need. Press q and more will exit.

Listing File Sizes

Now type ls -as. You can stack flags together like this-this tells ls to list all files, even hidden files, and list their sizes in kilobytes.

11.2.4 Logging Off

When you are finished you should be sure to logout! You need to be careful that you've typed logout correctly. The Unix operating system is not forgiving of mis-typed commands. Mis-typing logout as ``logotu'', pressing return and then leaving without glancing at the screen can leave your files at anyone's mercy.

11.3 Directory and File Structure

When you list files in Unix, it is very hard to tell what kind of files they are. The default behavior of the ls program is to list the names of all the files in the current directory without giving any additional information about whether they are text files, executable files or directories! This is because the ``meaning'' of the contents of each file is imposed on it by how you use the file. To the operating system a file is just a collection of bytes.

There is a program file which will tell you information about a file (such as whether it contains binary data) and make a good guess about what created the file and what kind of file it is.

11.3.1 File Names

Unlike other operating systems, filenames are not broken into a name part and a type part. Names can be many characters long and can contain most characters. Some characters such as * and ! have special meaning to the shell. They should not be used in filenames. If you ever do need to use such a symbol from the shell, they must be specified sneakily, by ``escaping'' them with a backslash, for example \!.

11.3.2 Directories

Directories in Unix start at the root directory ``/''. Files are ``fully specified'' when you list each directory branch needed to get to them.

/usr/local/lib/news

/home/pamela/src/file.c

The ``File System'' Tree Structure

Usually disks are ``partitioned'' into smaller sized sections called partitions If one partition of the disk fills up the other partitions won't be affected.

Only certain large directory points are partitions and the choice of these points can vary among system managers. Partitions are like the larger branches of a tree. Partitions will contain many smaller branches (directories) and leaves (files).

11.3.3 The df Program

To examine what disks and partitions exist and are mounted, you can type the df command at the % prompt. This should display partitions which have names like /dev/sd3g---3 for disk 3, g for partition g. It will also display the space used and available in kilobytes and the ``mount point'' or directory of the partition.

Disk Space Maintenance

It's important to keep track of how much disk space you are using. The command du displays the disk usage of the current directory and all of its subdirectories. It displays the usage, in kilobytes, for each directory-including any subdirectories it contains-and ends by displaying the total.
% du
    display disk usage of current directory
% du -s
    display only total disk usage
% du -s -k
    some versions of Unix need -k to report kilobytes

Scratch Space

Users have home directories for storing permanent files. At various busy times of the year there may be shortages of disk space on the Unix Cluster. You should use the du command to stay aware of how much space you are using and not exceed the system limits.

11.3.4 Your Login Directory

A login directory can always be specified with ~*username* (~ is commonly called ``twiddle,'' derived from proper term ``tilde.'') If you needed to list files in someone else's login directory, you could do so by issuing the command:

> % ls ~*username*

substituting in their username. You can do the same with your own directory if you've cd'd elsewhere. Please note-many people would consider looking at their files an invasion of their privacy; even if the files are not protected! Just as some people leave their doors unlocked but do not expect random bypassers to walk in, other people leave their files unprotected.

11.3.5 Subdirectories

If you have many files or multiple things to work on, you probably want to create subdirectories in your login directory. This allows you to place files which belong together in one distinct place.

Creating Subdirectories

The program to make a subdirectory is mkdir. If you are in your login directory and wish to create a directory, type the command:

> % mkdir *directory-name*

Once this directory has been created you can copy or move files to it (with the cp or mv programs) or you can cd to the directory and start creating files there.

Copy a file from the current directory into the new subdirectory by typing:

cp *filename directory-name*/ *new-filename*
> copy file, give it a new name

cp *filename directory-name*
> copy file, filename will be the same as original

Or cd into the new directory and move the file from elsewhere:

> % cd *directory-name*
> % cp ../*filename* .

copies the file from the directory above giving it the same filename: ``.'' means ``the current directory''

11.3.6 Specifying Files

There are two ways you can specify files. Fully, in which case the name of the file includes all of the root directories and starts with ``/'', or relatively, in which case the filename starts with the name of a subdirectory or consists solely of its own name.

When Charlotte Lennox (username lennox) created her directory arabella, all of the following sets of commands could be used to display the same file:

> % more lennox/arabella/chapter1

or

> % cd lennox
> % more arabella/chapter1

or
  % cd lennox/arabella
  % more chapter1
The full file specification, beginning with a ``/'' is very system dependent. On oceanography machines, all user directories are in the /usra partition.

      /usra/lennox/arabella/chapter1

11.3.7 Protecting Files and Directories

When created, all files have an owner and group associated with them. The owner is the same as the username of the person who created the files and the group is the name of the creator's default login group, such as users, system etc. Most users do not belong to a shared group on our systems. If the creator of the file belongs to more than one group (you can display the groups to which you belong with the groups command) then the creator can change the group of the file between these groups. Otherwise, only the root account can change the group of a file.

Only the root account can change the ownership of a file.

Displaying owner, group and protection

The command ls -lg*filename* will list the long directory list entry (which includes owner and protection bits) and the group of a file.

The display looks something like:

      protection owner   group   filename
      -rw-r----- hamilton ug   munster_village

The Protection Bits

The first position (which is not set) specifies what type of file this is. If it were set, it would probably be a d (for directory) or l (for link). The next nine positions are divided into three sets of binary numbers and determine protection to three different sets of people.

      u   g   o
      rw-   r--   ---
      6   4   0

The file has ``mode'' 640. The first bits, set to ``r + w'' (4+2) in our example, specify the protection for the user who owns the files (u). The user who owns the file can read or write (which includes delete) the file.

The next trio of bits, set to 4, or ``r,'' in our example, specify access to the file for other users in the same group as the group of the file. In this case the group is ug-all members of the ug group can read the file (print it out, copy it, or display it using more).

Finally, all other users are given no access to the file.

The one form of access which no one is given, even the owner, is ``x'' (for execute). This is because the file is not a program to be executed-it is probably a text file which would have no meaning to the computer. The x would appear in the 3rd position and have a value of 1.

Changing the Group and the Protection Bits

The group of a file can be changed with the chgrp command. Again, you can only change the group of a file to a group to which you belong. You would type as follows:

      % chgrp*groupname filename*

You can change the protection mode of a file with the chmod command. This can be done relatively or absolutely. The file in the example above had the mode 640. If you wanted to make the file readable to all other users, you could type:

    % chmod 644 *filename*
or
    % chmod +4 *filename*   (since the current mode of the file was 640)
For more information see the man page for chmod.

Default Protections: Setting the umask

All files get assigned an initial protection. To set the default initial protection you must set the value of the variable umask.umask must be defined once per login (usually in the .cshrc file). Common umask values include 022, giving read and directory search but not write permission to the group and others and 077 giving no access to group or other users for all new files you create.

11.3.8 The Unix Shell Syntax

As mentioned earlier, user commands are parsed by the shell they run. There are many shells other than the the C shell which allow different types of shortcuts. We will only discuss the C shell here, but some alternate shells include the Bourne shell (/bin/sh), the Bourne-Again Shell (bash), zsh and tcsh (a C shell variant).

The Path

One of the most important elements of the shell is the path. Whenever you type something at the % prompt, the C shell first checks to see if this is an ``alias'' you have defined, and if not, searches all the directories in your path to determine the program to run.

The path is just a list of directories, searched in order. Your default .cshrc will have a path defined for you. If you want other directories (such as a directory of your own programs) to be searched for commands, add them to your path by editing your .cshrc file. This list of directories is stored in the PATH environment variable. We will discuss how to manipulate enviroment variables later.

Flags and Parameters

Most commands expect or allow parameters (usually files or directories for the command to operate on) and many provide option flags. A ``flag'' as we saw before, is a character or string with a - before it-like the -s we used with the ls command.

Some commands, such as cp and mv require file parameters. Not surprisingly, cp and mv (the copy and move commands) each require two! One for the original file and one for the new file or location.

It would seem logical that if ls by itself just lists the current directory then cp*filename* should copy a file to the current directory. This is logical-but wrong! Instead you must enter cp*filename* . where the ``.'' tells cp to place the file in the current directory. *filename* in this case would be a long filename with a complete directory specification.

Not surprisingly ls . and ls are almost the same.

11.3.9 Creating Files

The cat Program

cat is one of most versatile commands. The simplest use of cat:

    % cat .cshrc

displays your .cshrc file to the screen. Unix allows you to redirect output which would otherwise go to the screen by using a > and a filename. You could copy your .cshrc, for example, by typing:

    % cat .cshrc > temp

This would have the same effect as:

    % cp .cshrc temp

More usefully cat will append multiple files together.

    % cat .cshrc .login > temp

will place copies of your .cshrc and .login into the same file. Warning! Be careful not to cat a file onto an existing file! The command:

    % cat .cshrc > .cshrc

will *destroy* the file .cshrc if it succeeds.

If you fail to give cat a filename to operate on, cat expects you to type in a file from the keyboard. You must end this with a <Ctrl>-D on a line by itself. <Ctrl>-D is the end-of-file character.

By combining these two-leaving off the name of a file to input to cat and telling cat to direct its output to a file with *>filename*, you can create files.

For example:

    % cat > temp

    ;klajs;dfkjaskj
    alskdj;kjdfskjdf
    <Ctrl>-D
    %

This will create a new file temp, containing the lines of garbage shown above. Note that this creates a new file-if you want to add things on to the end of an existing file you must use cat slightly differently. Instead of > you'd use >> which tells the shell to append any output to an already existing file. If you wanted to add a line onto your .cshrc, you could type

    % cat >> .cshrc
    echo "blah blah blah"
    <Ctrl>-D
    %

This would append the line echo "blah blah blah" onto your .cshrc. Using > here would be a bad idea-it might obliterate your original .cshrc file.

11.3.10 Text Editors

cat is fine for files which are small and never need to have real changes made to them, but a full-fledged editor is necessary for typing in papers, programs and mail messages. Among the editors available pico, vi and emacs.

Be careful! Not all Unix editors keep backup copies of files when you edit them.

pico

pico is a simple, friendly editor--the same editor as used in pine. Type pico*filename* to start it and type man pico for more information about how to use it.

Vi

vi is an editor which has a command mode and a typing mode. When you first startup vi (with the command vi*filename*) it expects you to enter commands. If you actually want to enter text into your file, you must type the insert command i. When you need to switch back to command mode, hit the escape key, usually in the upper left corner of your keyboard.

To move around you must be in command mode. You can use the arrow keys or use j, k, h, l to move down, up, left and right.

For more information type man vi. There are two reference sheets containing lists of the many vi commands available from C&C (located at Brooklyn and Pacific).

List of Commands for vi - An Unix Editor

Complete Documentation
The vi editor is a common editor for unix systems in that it makes use of a regular keyboard with an escape key. On the DECstation, the escape key is the F11 key. It therefore works on all unix computers. Complete documentation is available by typing

man vi

at the unix prompt.

Starting an Editing Session

vi filename

where *filename* is the name of the file to be edited.

Undo Command
u
   undo the last command.

Screen Commands
CTL/l
   Reprints current screen.
CTL/L
   Exposes one more line at top of screen.
CTL/E
   Exposes one more line at bottom of screen.
CTL/F
   Pages forward one screen.
CTL/B
   Pages back one screen.
CTL/D
   Pages down half screen.
CTL/U
   Pages up half screen.

Cursor Positioning Commands
j
   Moves cursor down one line, same column.
k
   Moves cursor up one line, same column.
h
   Moves cursor back one character.
l

Moves cursor forward one character.

RET

Moves cursor to beginning of next line.

0

Moves cursor to beginning of current line.

$

Moves cursor to end of current line.

SPACE

Moves cursor forward one character.

nG

Moves cursor to beginning of line n. Default is last line of file.

0

Moves the cursor to the first character of the line.

:n

Moves cursor to beginning of line n.

b

Moves the cursor backward to the beginning of the previous word.

e

Moves the cursor backward to the end of the previous word.

w

Moves the cursor forward to the next word.

/pattern

Moves cursor forward to next occurrence of *pattern*.

?pattern

Moves cursor backward to next occurrence of *pattern*.

n

Repeats last / or ? pattern search.

Text Insertion Commands

a

Appends text after cursor. Terminated by escape key.

A

Appends text at the end of the line. Terminated the escape key.

i

Inserts text before cursor. Terminated by the escape key.

I

Inserts text at the beginning of the line. Terminated by the escape key.

o

Opens new line below the current line for text insertion. Terminated by the escape key.

O

Opens new line above the current line for text insertion. Terminated by the escape key.

DEL

Overwrites last character during text insertion.

ESC

Stops text insertion. The escape key on the DECstations is the F11 key.

Text Deletion Commands

x

Deletes current character.

dd

Deletes current line.

dw

Deletes the current word.

d)

Deletes the rest of the current sentence.

D, d$

Deletes from cursor to end of line.

P

Puts back text from the previous delete.

Changing Commands

cw

    Changes characters of current word until stopped with escape key.

c$

    Changes text up to the end of the line.

C, cc

    Changes remaining text on current line until stopped by pressing the escape key.

~

    Changes case of current character.

xp

    Transposes current and following characters.

J

    Joins current line with next line.

s

    Deletes the current character and goes into the insertion mode.

r*x*

    Replaces current character with *x*.

R

    Replaces the following characters until terminated with the escape key.

Cut and Paste Commands

yy

    Puts the current line in a buffer. Does not delete the line from its current position.

p

    Places the line in the buffer after the current position of the cursor.

Appending Files into Current File

:R *filename*

    Inserts the file *filename* where the cursor was before the ``:" was typed.

Exiting vi

ZZ

    Exits vi and saves changes.

:wq

    Writes changes to current file and quits edit session.

:q!

    Quits edit session (no changes made).

Emacs

Emacs is a large editing system. Copies of the manual are for sale at the CCO Front Desk and copies of the two-page reference sheet are available in the reference sheet rack across from the Front Office.

To use emacs, type:

    % setup emacs
    % emacs

70

11.3.11 Files as Output and Log Files

Ordinarily there are two types of output from commands: output to standard output (stdout) and to standard error (stderr). The > and >> examples above directed only standard output from programs into files. To send both the standard output and error to a file when using the C shell, you should type >& :

>   %command>&filename

11.3.12 Logging Your Actions to a File

Sometimes you may wish to log the output of a login session to a file so that you can show it to somebody or print it out. You can do this with the script command. When you wish to end the session logging, type exit.

When you start up you should see a message saying script started, file is typescript and when you finish the script, you should see the message script done. You may want to edit the typescript file-visible ^M's get placed at the end of each line because linebreaks require two control sequences for a terminal screen but only one in a file.

11.3.13 Comparing Files

The basic commands for comparing files are:
cmp
          states whether or not the files are the same
diff
          lists line-by-line differences
comm
          three column output displays lines in file 1 only, file 2 only, and both files
See the man pages on these for more information.

11.3.14 Searching Through Files

The grep program can be used to search a file for lines containing a certain string:
>   % grep string filename
>   % grep -i string filename   (case insensitive match)
or not containing a certain string:

>   % grep -v string filename

See the man page for grep---it has many useful options.

more and the vi editor can also find strings in files. The command is the same in both-type a /string when at the --More-- prompt or in vi command mode. This will scroll through the file so that the line with ``string'' in it is placed at the top of the screen in more or move the cursor to the string desired in vi. Although vi is a text editor there is a version of vi,view, which lets you read through files but does not allow you to change them.

11.4 The System and Dealing with Multiple Users

Most Unix commands which return information about how much CPU-time you've used and how long you've been logged in use the following meanings for the words ``job'' and ``process.''

When you log in, you start an interactive "job" which lasts until you end it with the logout command. Using a shell like C shell which has "job-control" you can actually start jobs in addition to your login job. But for the purposes of the most information returning programs, job (as in the "JCPU" column) refers to your login session.

Processes, on the other hand, are much shorter-lived. Almost every time you type a command a new process is started. These processes stay "attached" to your terminal displaying output to the screen and, in some cases (interactive programs like text editors and mailers) accepting input from your keyboard.

Some processes last a very long time-for example the /bin/csh (C shell) process, which gets started when you login, lasts until you logout.

11.4.1 Information about Your Processes

You can get information about your processes by typing the ps command.
```
PID TT STAT  TIME COMMAND
9980 s9 S    0:06 -csh (csh)
12380 s9 R   0:01 ps
```
The processes executing above are the C shell process and the ps command. Note that both commands are attached to the same terminal (TT), have different process identification numbers (PID), and have different amounts of CPU-time (TIME), accumulated.

11.4.2 Information about Other People's Processes

who

The simplest and quickest information you can get about other people is a list of which users are logged in and at which "terminals" (terminal here is either a terminal device line or telnet or rlogin session). The command to do this is who and it responds quickest of all the commands discussed here because it simply examines a file which gets updated everytime someone logs in or out.

Be careful though! This file, utmp, can get out of date if someone's processes die unexpectedly on the system. Any program which uses utmp to report information may list users who are not really logged in!

w

The w command is slower than the who command because it returns more information such as details about what programs people are running. It also returns a line containing the number of users and the system load average. The load average is the average number of processes ready to be run by the CPU and is a rough way of estimating how busy a system is.

w also uses the utmp file mentioned above. It takes longer than who because it then looks around and collects more information about the users it finds in the utmp file.

ps

The ps command used earlier to list your own processes can be used to list other users' processes as well. who and w list logins-but not individual processes on the system. They don't list any of the running operating system processes which start when the computer is booted and which don't have logins.

Since ps doesn't use utmp it is the program to use when you really want to find out what processes you might have accidentally left on the system or if another user is running any processes. Note that although ps might report processes for a user, it might be because that user has left a ``background job'' executing. In this case you should see a ``?'' in the TT field and the user won't really be logged in.

To get this fuller listing, give the flags -aux to ps. For more information on the uses of ps, type man ps.

finger

The finger program returns information about other users on the system who may or may not be logged in. finger by itself returns yet another variation of the list of currently logged in users. finger followed by a username or an e-mail -style address will return information about one or more users, the last time they logged into the system where you are fingering them, their full name, whether or not they have unread mail and, finally, the contents of two files they may have created: .plan and .project

For more information about using finger or ways to provide information about yourself to others, type man finger.

11.5 Sending Messages and Files to Other Users

Electronic mail programs run on almost all the computers at Caltech and usually have two parts: a user interface which lets users read and send messages and a system mailer which talks to mailers on other computers. This mailer receives outgoing messages from the user interface programs and delivers incoming messages to the user mailbox (which the interface program reads).

11.5.1 /usr/ucb/mail

There are many user interfaces available on the Unix computers, all of which provide similar functionality. The program supplied with most Unix computers is /usr/ucb/mail (or Mail). To read messages type Mail, to send messages type:

    % Mail*address*

Mail has been changed to mailx.

You should next see a Subject: prompt. If you don't see a prompt, don't worry, just type in your one line subject anyway and press return. You may start typing your message (but you will be unable to correct errors on lines after you have pressed <CR> to move to the next line) or you may may specify a file to include with r*filename*.

You may invoke a text editor like vi by typing v. If you wish regularly to use an editor other than vi you should see the information later in this section about enviroment variables.

There are many other commands you may enter at this point-see the Mail man page for all of them. When you are finished typing in your message (if you have used v to run a text editor, you should exit from it) press <Ctrl>-D on a line by itself. Most likely you will now see a CC: prompt. If you wish to send copies of your message to someone besides the recipient you would enter the address or addresses (separated by ``,'') and press return. Otherwise press return without entering an address.

11.5.2 PINE

PINE is a full-screen interactive mailer, developed at UW, that is very straightforward to use. To use it type pine. More information is available from the UW C&C web server.

11.5.3 Write

The write program can be used to send messages to other users logged onto the system. It's not a great way of having a conversation, but it's simple to use. Enter:

% write*username*

and you can start writing lines to the terminal of the person you want to send messages to. The person must be logged in, and, if they are logged in more than once, you must specify the terminal to write to-for example write melville ttyh1.

11.5.4 Talk

talk is a program which allows two users to hold a conversation. Unlike write, it can be used between different computers; and, unlike write, it divides the screen so that the things you type appear in the top half and the things written to you appear in the bottom half.

To talk to users on the same computer:

% talk*username*

To talk to users on another computer use the address format of *username@nodename*:

% talk brunton@jarthur.claremont.edu

11.5.5 Addressing Remote Nodes

talk can only be used to other Internet nodes-computers which usually have ending names such as .edu, .com, .org, .gov, or .mil. Not all computers with these names are attached directly to the Internet--- finger and talk won't work with computers which are only attached by mail gateways.

11.6 Shortcuts

If you use certain command flags regularly (-lga for ls) you can alias them to shorter commands. You can use wildcard symbols to refer to files with very long names. You can easily repeat commands you have already executed or modify them slightly and re-execute them.

11.6.1 Aliases

As mentioned above, you can alias longer commands to shorter strings. For example, ls -F will list all the files in the current directory followed by a trailing symbol which indicates if they are executable commands (a *) or directories (a /). If you wanted this to be the default behavior of ls you could add the following command to your .cshrc:

% alias ls ls -F

To list the aliases which are set for your current process, type:

% alias

without any parameters.

11.6.2 Wildcards

Wildcards are special symbols which allow you to specify matches to letters or letter sequences as part of a filename.

Some examples:

*

The basic wildcard character. Beware rm *!!
ls *.dat
lists all files ending in .dat

ls r*
lists all files starting with r

?

a one character wildcard.
ls ?.dat
lists 5.dat, u.dat, but not 70.dat

[]

limits a character to match one of the characters between the brakets
ls *.[ch]
lists all .h and .c files
more [Rr][Ee][Aa][Dd][Mm][Ee]
mores the files README, readme,ReadMe, and Readme, among others

11.6.3 Directory Specifications

You've already met the shortcut. The two other important directory symbols are ``.'' for the current directory and ``..'' for the previous (parent) directory.

%% cd ..

moves you out of a subdirectory into its parent directory.

11.6.4 Environment Variables

Environment variables are pieces of information used by the shell and by other programs. One very important one is the PATH variable mentioned earlier. Other important variables you can set include:

- EDITOR
- TERM
- MAIL

To see what environment variables are set and what they are set to, type the command printenv. To set a variable, use the setenv command as in the example below.
%% setenv TERM vt100
%% setenv EDITOR emacs
Many programs mention environment variables you may want to set for them in their man pages. Look at the csh man page for some of the standard ones.

11.6.5 History

Most shells allow ``command line editing'' of some form or another-editing one of the previous few lines you've typed in and executing the changed line. You can set a history ``environment variable'' to determine how many previous command lines you will have access to with set history=40

Repeating and Modifying the Previous Command

The simplest form of command line editing is to repeat the last command entered or repeat the last command entered with more text appended.

If the last command you typed was:

%% ls agreen

Then you can repeat this command by typing:

%% !!

This will return a list of files. If you saw a directory leavenworth in the list returned and you wanted to list the files it contained, you could do so by typing:

% !!/leavenworth

If you mistype leavenworth as leaveworth you can correct it with the following command:

% ^leave^leaven

This substitutes leaven for leave in the most recently executed command. Beware! This substitutes for the *first* occurrence of leave only!

Repeating Commands From Further Back in History

You can type history at any time to get a list of all the commands remembered. This list is numbered and you can type ! *number* to repeat the command associated with number. Alternately you can type ! and a couple of letters of the command to repeat the last line starting with the characters you specify. !ls to repeat ls -lgagreen, for example.

11.6.6 The .login and .cshrc Files

The .cshrc file is run whenever a C shell process is started. Then, if this is a login process, the .login file is executed. If you are using a NeXT console with a program such as Terminal, you can usually choose whether you want each new window to execute the .login file by making a change to your Preferences in the Terminal program's Preferences menu. By default the .login will get executed.

If you are using a Sun console and you have the default setup, any xterm windows which you start up will not execute the .login.

11.7 Job Control

It is very easy to do many things at once with the Unix operating system. Since programs and commands execute as independent processes you can run them in the ``background" and continue on in the foreground with more important tasks or tasks which require keyboard entry.

For example, you could set a program running in the background while you edit a file in the foreground.

11.7.1 The fg and bg Commands

When you type <Ctrl>-Z whatever you were doing will pause. If you want the job to go away without finishing, then you should kill it with the command kill %. If you don't want it paused but want it to continue in the foreground-that is, if you want it to be the primary process to which all the characters you type get delivered-type fg. If you want it to continue processing in the background while you work on something else, type bg.

You should not use bg on things which accept input such as text editors or on things which display copious output like more or ps.

What to Do When You've Suspended Multiple Jobs

If you've got several processes stopped-perhaps you are editing two files or you have multiple telnet or rlogin sessions to remote computers-you'll need some way of telling fg which job you want brought to the foreground.

By default fg will return you to the process you most recently suspended. If you wanted to switch processes you would have to identify it by its job number. This number can be displayed with the jobs command. For example:

```
% jobs
[1]        Stopped    vi .login
[2]    +   Stopped    rn
[3]        Running    cc -O -g test.c
%
```

The most recently suspended job is marked with a + symbol. If you wanted to return to job one instead, you would type:

```
% fg %1
```

You can type %1 as a shortcut.

11.7.2 Starting Jobs in the Background

Some jobs should start in the background and stay there-long running compilations or programs, for example. In this case you can direct them to the background when you start them rather than after they have already begun. To start a job in the background rather than the foreground, append an & symbol to the end of your command.

You should always run background processes at a lower priority by using the nice command. Non-interactive jobs are usually very good at getting all the resources they need. Running them at a lower priority doesn't hurt them much-but it *really* helps the interactive users-people running programs that display to terminal screens or that require input from the keyboard.

If you need to run CPU-intensive background jobs, learn about how to control the priority of your jobs by reading the manual pages (man nice and man renice).

Suspend, z and <Ctrl>-Z

Some programs provide you with special ways of suspending them. If you started another shell by using the csh command, you would have to use the suspend command to suspend it.

If you wish to suspend a telnet or rlogin session you must first get past the current login to get the attention of the telnet or rlogin program.

Use (immediately after pressing a return) to get rlogin's attention. <Ctrl>-Z will suspend an rlogin session.

Use <Ctrl>-] to get telnet's attention <Ctrl>-]z will suspend a telnet session. Watch out, though, if you are connected from a PC with through Kermit! <Ctrl>-] is Kermit's default escape sequence. You'll need to type <Ctrl>-] z or define Kermit's escape sequence to something else such as <Ctrl>-K.

11.8 Some Common and Useful Unix Commands For Files

cp

The cp command allows you to create a new file from an existing file. The command line format is:

```
% cpinput-file-spec output-file-spec
```

where *input-file-spec* and *output-file-spec* are valid Unix file specifications. The file specifications indicate the file(s) to copy from and the file or directory to copy to (output). Any part of the filename may be replaced by a wildcard symbol (*) and you may specify either a filename or a directory for the *output-file-spec*. If you do not specify a directory, you should be careful that any wildcard used in the *input-file-spec* does not cause more than one file to get copied.

```
% cp new.c old.c
% cp new.* OLD (where OLD is a directory)
```

ls

command allows the user to get a list of files in the current default directory. The command line format is:

% ls*file-spec-list*

where *file-spec-list* is an optional parameter of zero or more Unix file specifications (separated by spaces). The file specification supplied (if any) indicates which directory is to be listed and the files within the directory to list.

lpr

The lpr command tells the system that one or more files are to be printed on the default printer. If the printer is busy with another user's file, an entry will be made in the printer queue and the file will be printed after other lpr requests have been satisfied. The command line format is:

BLOCKQUOTE>% lpr*file-spec-list*

where *file-spec-list* is one or more Unix files to be printed on the default printer. Any part of the filenames may be replaced by a wild card.

Here is more information about where the printers actually are and what kind of printers are available.

man

The man command is a tool that gives the user brief descriptions of Unix commands along with a list of all of the command flags that the command can use. To use man, try one of the following formats:
% man *command*
% man -k *topic*

more

The more command will print the contents of one or more files on the user's terminal. The command line format is:

% more *file-spec-list*

more displays a page at a time, waiting for you to press the space-bar at the end of each screen. At any time you may type q to quit or h to get a list of other commands that more understands.

mv

The mv command is used to move files to different names or directories. The command line syntax is:

% mv*input-file-spec output-file-spec*

where *input-file-spec* is the file or files to be renamed or moved. As with cp, if you specify multiple input files, the output file should be a directory. Otherwise *output-file-spec* may specify the new name of the file. Any or all of the filename may be replaced by a wild card to abbreviate it or to allow more than one file to be moved. For example:

% mv data.dat ./research/datadat.old

will change the name of the file data.dat to datadat.old and place it in the subdirectory research. Be very careful when copying or moving multiple files.

rm

The rm command allows you to delete one or more files from a disk. The command line format is:

% rm*file-spec-list*

where *file-spec-list* is one or more Unix file specifications, separated by spaces, listing which files are to be deleted. Beware of rm *! For example:

% rm *.dat able.txt

will delete the file able.txt and all files in your current working directory which end in .dat. Getting rid of unwanted subdirectories is a little more difficult. You can delete an empty directory with the command rmdir*directory-name* but you cannot use rmdir to delete a directory that still has files in it.

To delete a directory with files in it, use rm with the -r flag (for recursive).

www.ingramcontent.com/pod-product-compliance
Lightning Source LLC
Chambersburg PA
CBHW060323220326
41598CB00027B/4406